101
Teambuilding
Activities

101

Teambuilding
Activities

Ideas Every Coach Can Use
to Enhance Teamwork,
Communication and Trust

Greg Dale, Ph.D.
Scott Conant, M.A.

Cover design by Through the Moon Editorial and Publishing Services, LLC.
Cover photo: www.comstock.com

Published by Excellence in Performance
7 Sinclair Circle Durham, NC 27705
www.excellenceinperformance.com
gdale@duke.edu
(919) 401-9640

Production assistance from
Through the Moon Editorial and Publishing Services, LLC.
Info@throughthemoon.com | (919) 643-2968
www.throughthemoon.com

If you are unable to order this book from your local
bookseller, you may order directly from the publisher.
gdale@duke.edu | (919) 401-9640

Library of Congress Control Number: 2004108061
ISBN-13: 978-0-9755764-1-0
10 9 8 7
Printed on acid free paper in the USA.

Dedications

To my family: Cammie, Abbey, Graham and Jacob. Thanks for all your support during the process of writing this book.

—Greg Dale

To Rebekah for her love and unconditional support. To Cale, Cliff, Carrie and René for always making life interesting and a learning experience.

—Scott Conant

Table of Contents

Photo Credits xi

Acknowledgments 1

Introduction 3

Initiatives

1. Someone Who Made a Difference 12
2. Sharing Personal Stories 13
3. Most Embarrassing and Proudest Moments 14
4. Two Truths and a Lie 15
5. Personal Legacy 16
6. Scrambled Eggs 17
7. Number Line 18
8. The Game is On! 19
9. Bizz-Buzz 20
10. I-So-Co 21

Championship-Level Environment

11. Team Retreats 24
12. Team *Jeopardy* 25
13. Skit Night 26
14. Team Culture Debate 27
15. Commitment Contract 28
16. Who Are the People in Our Neighborhood? 29
17. Maintaining a Good Balance 30
18. Role Appreciation Cards 31
19. Changing Roles 32
20. Commitment Cards 33
21. Team Council Meeting 34
22. Our Team Is Like a Hand 35
23. These Shoes Were Made for Talking 36
24. Team Symbol 37

25. Big Brother/Big Sister Program 38
26. Notes from Coach 39
27. Establishing a Culture of "Toughness" 40
28. Role-Play Dealing with Adversity 41
29. What My Coach Can Do to Motivate Me 42
30. What My Teammates Can Do to Motivate Me 43
31. Athletes Planning and Conducting Practice 44
32. Alter Ego 45
33. Athletes Responsible for Scouting Report 46
34. Athletes Providing Each Other with Feedback 47
35. Athletes Evaluating Your Program 48

Trust

36. You Can Count on Me 52
37. Leap of Faith 53
38. Can I Trust You? 54
39. Trusting Our Leaders 55
40. I Can Carry You on My Back 56
41. Mouse Trap Trust 57
42. Ball of String 58

Communication

43. Team Telephone 62
44. The "Voice" of the Team 63
45. Mine Field 64
46. Squeeze Play 65
47. Lightning-Fast 66
48. Word String 67
49. Barnyard Music 68
50. Build the Court 70
51. Team Support 72
52. Team Blob 73

Teamwork

53. Keeper in the Cage 76
54. Wacky Baseball 78
55. Balloon Challenge 79

56. Reverse-Order Stepping-Stones 80
57. Stretching It 81
58. Alligator Pond 82
59. Activity Buddy 83
60. Problem-Solving 84
61. Shoestring Challenge 86
62. Yurt Circle 87
63. Team Web 88
64. Inner Tube Challenge 89
65. Balloon Train 90
66. Team Juggle 91
67. Flip Flop 92
68. Blind Spell 93
69. Tin Can Transfer 94
70. Dependent Pairs Tag 95
71. Team Pyramid 96
72. Spokes in the Wheel 97
73. Bungee Challenge 98
74. Balance 99
75. Navigating Obstacles 100
76. Team Tag 101
77. Balloon Tower 102
78. Tug O' War 103
79 Photo Scavenger Hunt 104
80. Pigpen 106
81. Team Lunches 107
82. Team Dinners 108
83. Team Road Races 109
84. Team Transport 110
85. You Want *How Much* Playing Time? .111
86. Team Limbo 112
87. Service Project 113
88. Potato Relay 114
89. Water Relay 115
90. Tissue Race 116
91. Banana Relay 117
92. Inchworm Relay 118
93. Hoop Relay 119

94. Potato Chip Relay 120
95. Belly Ball Relay 121
96. Team Olympics 122

Adventure-Based Activities

97. High Ropes 126
98. Camping Trip 127
99. Hiking or Mountain Climbing 128
100.White-Water Rafting 130
101.Caving Experience 131

Coaching Staff Activities

Retreats 134
Ropes Course 134
Switch Positions 134
Switch Teams 135
Family Night 135
Treat Members of Staff with Respect 135
Allow the Staff to Provide You with Feedback 136

Conclusion 137

About the Authors 138

Workshops by Greg Dale 140

Photo Credits

Acknowledgments

Greg would like to thank several people for their assistance with this project. Thanks to Trip Hedrick for his initial support for the idea. Thanks to Cammie Dale, Dawn Kerr and in particular Shelley Johnson for their editorial suggestions throughout the process. Thanks to Scott Yakola for his assistance with the photos. Finally, thanks to all of the coaches and others who allowed us to share their teambuilding ideas.

Scott would like to thank all those who have influenced him through Experiential Education and Adventure.

Introduction

"Individual commitment to a group effort—that is what makes a team work, a company work, a society work, a civilization work."

—Vince Lombardi, Former Coach, Green Bay Packers

The fact that you have picked this book up and have begun reading it indicates you are at least somewhat intrigued by team dynamics and factors that contribute to or detract from it. There is significant variation in the amount of time and effort coaches spend on developing teamwork, communication, trust and positive team environment with their teams. Some coaches win a lot of games despite spending very little time focusing on the environment in and around their teams. Their focus tends to revolve around strategy and technique. A college basketball coach once said, "I don't have time to spend working on team dynamics, team cohesion or whatever you want to call it. I need to focus on teaching these guys the skills that will help them execute well when it is time to play. Besides, athletes will only use 'a lack of team cohesion and trust' as an excuse when things aren't going well." Part of the reason coaches such as this succeed in terms of wins and losses could be because they are able to coach very highly motivated and committed athletes who would most likely excel in any environment. But the question becomes how much more successful could their teams be if they spent more time and energy on these aspects of their team? There are countless research studies and undeniable anecdotal evidence to demonstrate that teams which have athletes who communicate well with each other, trust each other, get along with each other reasonably well and embrace a championship team environment perform better than teams that do not possess these qualities.

Fortunately, there are many coaches who do see the importance of spending time on teambuilding and talk to athletes about its importance on a regular basis—sometimes daily. You could be one of those coaches. You might spend a great deal of time talking to your team about the importance of the "intangibles" that sometimes make the difference between success and failure. While it is important to continually discuss these keys to success, we have found that athletes who participate in activities which move beyond mere discussion are more likely to retain the message and apply what they learn to competition. Ian Boyle illustrates this very well in his 2002 dissertation (see reference, p. 131), when he writes that we remember 20 percent of what we hear, 50 percent of what we see and 80 percent of what we do. With this in mind, we have set out to provide you with a variety of activities that will allow your athletes to experience the concepts of teamwork, communication and trust. These concepts will come alive as your athletes participate in fun, interactive and challenging games and activities.

Some of the activities in this book will be more effective during the preseason when you are trying to help team members learn more about each other and you are laying a foundation of trust and camaraderie. Some of the activities will be more beneficial during the season to help you more effectively make a point about the importance of certain aspects of team success such as communication, trust or teamwork. Sometimes your team will be struggling with one particular area, and these activities will serve as a great reinforcement for what you say about its importance for the team's success. Finally, on occasion, your team will be experiencing fatigue and potential burnout toward the end of a long season. Many of these activities can serve as a fun and meaningful break from the traditional grind of practice. Your athletes will appreciate the variety and will most likely learn valuable lessons in the process.

So, we encourage you to read through this book with an open mind. Just as you often ask your athletes to expand their comfort zones, you might have to stretch your comfort zone and incorporate these activities into your repertoire of teaching aids. Be willing to try these activities with your athletes—even the ones you feel might not apply. You might be pleasantly surprised!

Layout of the Book

All of the activities in the book fall into one or more of the following categories. The categories are not mutually exclusive, as many activities apply to several categories.

Initiatives—Activities in this area provide avenues for athletes on your team to get to know their teammates away from the sport. Many of the activities require athletes to take risks and open themselves up to their teammates. You will find these activities to be most useful at the beginning of preseason, when many of your athletes are unfamiliar with each other.

Championship-Level Team Environment—Activities in this area highlight the impact of embracing a certain team culture. Athletes will be challenged to not only think about the type of culture they want to have on their team, but will learn strategies to help them "live" that culture on a daily basis.

Trust—Activities in this area demonstrate the power of trust among teammates. Some activities will require athletes to disclose information that is personal in nature. Similar to activities on teamwork, some of these activities will require athletes to trust that their teammates will do their parts to successfully reach a goal. Processing these activities afterwards will provide direct references to the importance of trust and accountability away from the sport, as well as when athletes are competing together.

Communication—Activities in this area reinforce the importance of every member of a team communicating effectively. Athletes participating in these activities will further their understanding of the communication process. They will experience the satisfaction of accomplishing a task because of effective communication, as well as the consequences of breakdowns in communication among teammates.

Teamwork—Activities in this area provide experiences that require athletes to work together to accomplish a specific goal. Most activities highlight the importance of accountability among teammates and the concept that the team needs each athlete to perform his or her role at a high level. In essence, these activities reinforce the phrase, "A chain is only as strong as its weakest link."

Adventure-Based Activities—Activities in this area will require athletes to expand their comfort zones and challenge them to succeed in difficult situations. Many athletes on your team will not have participated in these types of activities and will be somewhat apprehensive. But after experiencing these activities as part of a team, athletes will likely have a different perspective on challenging situations and demonstrate a higher level of self-confidence.

Coaching Staff—Activities in this area provide ideas to enhance teamwork, communication, trust and a positive team environment among the staff. While the activities are not necessarily experiential in nature, they do provide specific ideas on ways to enhance the way the staff works as a team of coaches.

Description of the Activities

With the exception of the activities intended for the coaching staff, all activities are presented in the same format throughout the book. By presenting the activities in this format, we hoped to keep it simple and limit technical jargon. The following is a brief discussion of the various sections contained in the description of each activity.

GOAL

This is the main objective the activity will help you accomplish. As you use these activities with your teams, you will realize there can be several goals for one activity.

NUMBERS

This indicates the "ideal" number of athletes that can effectively participate in a particular activity. We often indicate that you should break the team into smaller teams or subunits if you have a large team. By doing this, you will allow all of your athletes to participate and it can further unity among certain subunits on the team. Use the numbers we suggest as a guide; there are many ways to creatively adapt to the actual numbers on your team.

EQUIPMENT

Here we indicate the type and amount of equipment you will need to successfully conduct this activity. We made every attempt to include activities in the book that required little or no equipment. Most of the activities can be conducted using equipment that is commonplace in most athletic departments. You will have to invest some money to buy small items such as blindfolds and balloons for some of the activities. Many of the items can be used repeatedly. Some activities will require more of a financial commitment, such as paying for team trips. This money could be secured from your booster club, fees from the athletes or through fund-raisers. Coaches tend to be very creative when it comes to raising money, and these activities will be well worth any money you must invest.

SPACE

This indicates the physical space you will need to conduct the activity. Except for a few of the **Adventure-Based Activities**, you will be able to use your practice or competition facility. Some activities require that you have a hard surface such as basketball or volleyball floor.

SAFETY

This is clearly the most important section in the description of each activity. It is imperative that you always keep the safety of your athletes first and foremost when conducting any of the activities in this book. It is certainly best to err on the side of caution than to take unnecessary risks with the safety of your athletes. With that said, the overwhelming majority of the activities are very safe when athletes and coaches use common sense. Some **Adventure-Based Activities** will require that you enlist the assistance of professionally trained and qualified personnel. Always make sure the individual or company you use has a very good safety record.

GAME PLAN

This is the space where we describe the activity. We make every attempt to be as descriptive as possible with the protocol and rules of the activity while still being concise. This description is intended to be a guide to help you design the activity, but there will be times that you will need to make modifications to accommodate your team. You can present the activity in simple terms by merely telling the team the facts of what they have to do to be successful. You can be creative when introducing the activities to your athletes by creating an imaginary scenario such as the team has to cross an alligator pond without anyone getting bitten. Or you can present the activity in a way that it directly relates to the team's current situation, right from the very beginning of the activity, rather than waiting until the wrap-up session. Whatever way you decide to present the activity, it is important to present it with enthusiasm.

WRAP-UP

Without a proper wrap-up, these activities will serve little more purpose than as an opportunity for your athletes to laugh at themselves and have fun. While fun is a goal for all of these activities, the potential for much greater meaning and relevance is present in all cases. It is very important that you are able to move beyond your role as coach and become more of a facilitator during this phase of the activity. We provide you a series of questions or prompts for every activity. Once again, this material is provided merely as a guide to facilitate the lessons and application of each activity to sport and your team. A key to the success of an activity will be your ability to get athletes to see how it relates to the success of their team. To accomplish this, you will need to be aware of, and avoid, the tendency to "lead" your athletes into thinking what you want them to think about an activity or what you feel is the "real" experience they should take from it. It will be their experience rather than yours. In addition, you will need to create an atmosphere where athletes trust you and are willing to freely discuss their experiences and frustrations as a result of participating in an activity. You can accomplish this by not judging athletes for their honesty or holding anything against an athlete after an activity is finished. If this is difficult for you, it might be a good idea to have someone experienced in facilitating these types of activities to take your team through the process as you observe.

VARIATIONS

We attempted to provide you with variations for many of the activities in the book. These variations are either ones that we have used or that other coaches have found to be successful. You will find that you will be able to create many other variations as you conduct these activities with your teams through the years. You will have different athletes on teams with different issues that will need to be addressed. We only ask that you let us know if you come up with a variation that works well so we can include it in the next edition. You can send those variations to Greg at **gdale@duke.edu**.

Reference

Many of the activities are ones we have used with teams or have observed coaches use. Some of the activities were graciously provided by other coaches and sport psychology consultants. Finally, several of the activities are variations of those found in other books. Every attempt has been made to properly reference each activity in this book.

Disclaimer

The activities in this book are designed to be interactive, fun and relevant to issues athletes face in competitive team situations, but can present physical and emotional challenges for the athletes who participate in them. Athletes should always be given the choice as to whether they would like to participate and should never be unduly coerced to participate. The descriptions of these activities are meant to serve merely as a guide to you and/or anyone else who might lead or participate in them in any manner. It is up to the leader to determine the appropriateness of an activity before allowing any athletes to engage in it. Common sense should always be used when conducting experiential and adventure-based activities, and the safety of your athletes should be paramount in every situation. The authors and publisher are not responsible and assume no liability for any actions taken by anyone who leads or participates in any of the activities presented in this book.

The Use of "He" and "She"

All activities in this book have been successfully carried out with both male and female athletes. Every attempt has been made throughout the book to represent both gender groups by using "he" and "she" when describing these activities. For the sake of readability, "he/she" is not used.

Initiatives

Someone Who Made a Difference

Goal
Identify and reflect on a person who has made a difference in your life.

Numbers
No limit. Consider dividing athletes into smaller subunits if more than 20.

Equipment
None.

Space
Use any space where athletes will not be disturbed.

Safety
N/A.

Game Plan
This is an activity that gives athletes an opportunity to learn about their team-mates and a significant person in their lives. Begin the activity by telling your athletes that most all of us have had someone that has helped us along our journeys in some capacity. Encourage your athletes to reflect on a person that made a significant difference in their lives and helped shape the people they are today. After allowing ample time for everyone to identify someone, allow each athlete the opportunity to share with the team why this person is significant.

Wrap-Up
Why do you think it is important to reflect on someone who is special in your life? Do you ever let this person know how much he or she means to you?

Variations
You can do this activity at a time during the season when you feel your team could use a little extra inspiration. You can have athletes write the name of their significant person somewhere in their locker or on a piece of equipment, so that person can serve as an inspiration when the athletes are experiencing difficulties on or off the playing field. Members of the University of Michigan Field Hockey team have written the initials of that person on their hands. If the person that was chosen is not deceased, you can encourage athletes to tell this person how much of a difference he or she has made. Preferably, they would do it in person, but calling or writing can be very effective as well.

Sharing Personal Stories

Goal
Encourage the development of trust among team members.

Numbers
No limit. Consider dividing athletes into smaller subunits if more than 20.

Equipment
None.

Space
Use any space where athletes will not be disturbed.

Safety
N/A.

Game Plan
This is a great trust-building activity that can be done very early in the pre-season. Each team member is asked to share a personal story about themselves that few people know. It should be a story about an event or events in their lives that shaped who they are at the current time.

Wrap-Up
What was it like to share that experience?
What happens on a team when team members are willing to share stories like this with each other?

Variations
Have athletes draw a picture that depicts the event. The picture will provide a visual to accompany the storytelling. It will also demonstrate their artistic ability or lack thereof.

MOST EMBARRASSING AND PROUDEST MOMENTS

GOAL
Encourage the development of trust among team members.

NUMBERS
No limit. Consider dividing athletes into smaller subunits if more than 20.

EQUIPMENT
None.

SPACE
Use any space where athletes will not be disturbed.

SAFETY
Team members should be encouraged to avoid judging team members based on the stories they tell.

GAME PLAN
Provide each member of the team with two pieces of paper. Team members should draw a picture of the moment in their lives where they were the proudest. Upon finishing this drawing, team members should draw a picture of their most embarrassing moment. Once everyone is finished drawing, team members should take turns sharing their most embarrassing moments. After everyone is finished, team members should share their most proud moments. The team will have fun participating in this exercise and it will provide further insight into each member of the team.

WRAP-UP
Did you learn anything new about any of your teammates?
What surprised you the most?
How might this exercise help you trust your teammates?
Why is it important to divulge your most embarrassing moment?

VARIATIONS
Have team members talk about the moments without drawing them.

TWO TRUTHS AND A LIE

GOAL
Allow team members to get to know one another better.

NUMBERS
No limit. Consider dividing athletes into smaller subunits if more than 20.

EQUIPMENT
None.

SPACE
Use any space where athletes will not be disturbed.

SAFETY
N/A.

GAME PLAN
This is an activity that allows athletes to have fun while getting to know each other better. Each team member is allowed 3-4 minutes to think of three experiences or aspects of their lives they would like to share with their teammates. Two of these experiences/aspects should be truths. A third should be a lie. Once everyone is ready, team members should take turns sharing their experiences. As each team member finishes, the rest of the team or subunit should guess which one was a lie.

WRAP-UP
Did you learn anything new about any of your teammates?
What surprised you the most?

VARIATIONS
Athletes could tell one truth and two lies and have teammates guess which is the truth.
Have athletes write their responses on small slips of paper, place them in a container and then pull slips of paper from the container one at a time. Read them aloud and have everyone try to guess which athlete wrote that information.
Involve the coaching staff in this activity by having them tell about themselves.

Contributed by Bob "Bumpa" Town, Cleveland, Ohio.

PERSONAL LEGACY

GOAL
Allow each athlete on the team to think about what his or her legacy will be at the end of the season.

NUMBERS
No limit. Consider dividing athletes into smaller subunits if more than 20.

EQUIPMENT
None.

SPACE
Locker room, on the practice or playing surface, a classroom, a road trip or a camping trip.

SAFETY
N/A.

GAME PLAN
This activity should be conducted early in the year. You can set this activity up by telling your athletes to think about the end of the year banquet and that each of them will have a representative from three groups to talk about his legacy during the year. Athletes should think about what they want their team-mates, coaches and opponents to say about them at the banquet. Once you have given all athletes ample time to devise a proposed legacy, ask each athlete to share his projected legacy with the rest of the team or subunit. Each athlete should also be required to indicate what he will do on a daily basis to "live his legacy" throughout the year.

WRAP-UP
What was it like to have to share these thoughts with your teammates?
How can you help each other live up to the legacies that were mentioned?
What can the coaching staff do to help each athlete live up to the desired legacy?

VARIATIONS
Have athletes write these desired legacies down on paper and post them in their lockers or somewhere they can be constantly reminded of what they said at the beginning of the year.
Conduct this activity for each of the seasons in your sport (e.g., preseason, in-season and off-season).

SCRAMBLED EGGS

GOAL
Allow teammates an opportunity to get to know one another during a simple activity that requires communication and teamwork.

NUMBERS
No limit. Divide team into smaller subunits of 6-10 athletes if it is a large team.

EQUIPMENT
None.

SPACE
A flat area that is free of obstacles.

SAFETY
No horseplay.

GAME PLAN
This is a great activity for creating an environment where athletes must invade the personal space of their teammates. Begin the activity by putting team members into teams of 6-10. Once in teams, each athlete should put one hand in the middle of the circle and hold another athlete's hand. Then each team member puts his other hand in the middle and holds a different athlete's free hand. Athletes are not permitted to hold the hand of the person next to them in the circle. The objective is for each team to untie themselves without anyone letting go of hands. You can have teams compete to see which team can untie their knot the fastest, or you can simply time them if you have one team.

WRAP-UP
What happened during that activity?
Did everyone have to contribute in some way?
What did you do when you got stuck or didn't know what to do next?
How might this activity apply to what we will have to do as a team?

VARIATIONS
Blindfold a few of the athletes from each team to increase the challenge.

NUMBER LINE

GOAL
Encourage risk-taking, communication and pursuit of a difficult goal.

NUMBERS
8-20 is ideal. Consider dividing team into smaller subunits if more than 20.

EQUIPMENT
Blindfold for each athlete.

SPACE
A flat area that is free of any obstacles.

SAFETY
No horseplay.
All movement should be slow and team members must stand in an upright position.

GAME PLAN
This activity will require athletes to be creative and use alternative modes of communication to accomplish a task. Begin by asking athletes to stand with their team in a circle and put on their blindfolds. Inform athletes they are not allowed to talk at any time during this activity. Remind them that safety is very important during the activity as they will not be able to see or talk. Once everyone has put on a blindfold, you can then give each team member a number by whispering it or by tapping the number in her hand. After everyone has a number, mix the team up by moving everyone around. Then tell athletes that they must form a straight line in numerical order (e.g., 1-12). Again, remind them to avoid talking to any of their teammates as they begin this activity.

WRAP-UP
Did any of you ever think this activity was impossible?
Was this activity ever frustrating?
How did you figure out how to accomplish the goal?
What forms of communication does this team have to do in order to be successful?

VARIATION
Have the team get in line according to birthdays, shoe size, alphabetically by name or any other creative manner.

THE GAME IS ON!

GOAL
Allow athletes to get to know more about their teammates.

NUMBERS
13-19 is ideal. Divide team into smaller subunits if more than 19. Keep in mind that this activity will work best if you have an odd number of athletes participating.

EQUIPMENT
Hula Hoops or markers to signify where athletes sit.

SPACE
Area free of obstacles and about half the size of a basketball court.

SAFETY
Athletes must be careful to avoid tripping teammates.

GAME PLAN
This activity is similar to the old favorite, Musical Chairs. Begin the activity by placing Hula Hoops or other markers on the floor in a large circle. Once the markers are on the floor, athletes should get a partner and sit back to back inside a hoop. One athlete should be designated to be in the middle of the circle. This athlete begins the activity by saying, "The game is on for ..." and finish this sentence by saying something that is true about herself. For example, she can say, "The game is on for anyone with two siblings" or "The game is on for anyone born in December." Everyone on the team that this statement pertains to must get up from their seats and run around the circle in the same direction to fill an open position in the circle that has been vacated by someone for whom "the game is on." The last athlete standing must go to the middle and come up with a new way to finish the phrase.

WRAP-UP
Did you learn something new about any of your teammates? If so, what did you learn?

From Aynsley Smith, *Powerplay: Mental Toughness for Hockey and Beyond* (Athletic Guide Publishing: Flagler Beach, Florida, 1999).

BIZZ-BUZZ

GOAL
Allow athletes to see the importance of concentration and teamwork.

NUMBERS
Divide team into groups of 6-10.

EQUIPMENT
None.

SPACE
Locker room, classroom or the practice or playing surface.

SAFETY
N/A.

GAME PLAN
Divide your team into groups of 6-10 people, and have each group get into a circle facing each other. The object of this activity is for each circle of athletes to count as high as they can without saying the number 7, a number with 7 in it (e.g., 17, 47) or a multiple of 7 (e.g., 21, 35). The following guidelines should be followed when participating in this activity:

> One person should be designated to begin the counting sequence.
>
> That person begins with the number 1.
>
> Going clockwise, the next person says the number 2.
>
> This sequence continues until the number 7.
>
> The athlete who is supposed to say the number "7" must instead say "bizz" or "buzz."
>
> If the athlete says "bizz," the counting continues in a clockwise manner.
>
> If the athlete says "buzz," the counting continues in a counter-clockwise manner.
>
> In either case, the next person must say the number 8 and the sequence continues until a number with 7 in or a multiple of 7 is replaced by either "bizz" or "buzz."
>
> The team must start over each time there is a mistake or hesitation of any length.

WRAP-UP
What happened when one of your teammates made a mistake and your team had to begin again?

Can anyone discuss what happened when you thought it would be your turn to say "bizz" or "buzz" as your team progressed to higher numbers?

How might this apply to us when we are competing?

VARIATIONS
One team can stand outside the circle of a team that is participating in the activity and attempt to verbally distract them. The team participating will have to ignore them and perform effectively without making a mistake.

From Karl Rohnke and Steve Butler, *Quicksilver* (Kendall/Hunt Publishing: Dubuque, Iowa, 1995).

I-So-Co

GOAL
Allow athletes to see the importance of concentration and teamwork.

NUMBERS
No limit. Divide team into groups of 6-10 if the team is large.

EQUIPMENT
None.

SPACE
Locker room, a classroom or the practice or playing surface.

SAFETY
N/A.

GAME PLAN
Divide your team into groups of 6-10 people, and have each group get into a circle with members facing each other. The object of the game is for athletes to play this game using hand signals and saying the nonsensical phrases "I," "So" or "Co" without making an error. Each group should see how long it can progress without anyone making a mistake. The following guidelines should be followed when participating in this activity:

One person should be designated to begin the activity by saluting across his or her forehead (similar to a military salute) to either the right or left while simultaneously saying "I."

If the salute is made with the right hand, the person to the immediate left must bring either arm across the chest as if saluting while simultaneously saying "So." Depending on the direction of this salute, the person to the left or right must clasp both hands together, point to someone across the circle and simultaneously say "Co."

That person begins the whole process again, saying "I."

Let each group practice several times and then tell them "from now on, it really counts." Watch for their reactions when you put a little pressure on them by telling them it is more important now.

WRAP-UP
What happened during this activity?
What was your reaction when one of your teammates made a mistake?
What was your reaction when you made a mistake?
How might this apply to us when we are competing?

VARIATIONS
Once an athlete makes a mistake, he or she can go outside the circle and attempt to distract others in the group. The circle becomes smaller as athletes make mistakes. The last two or three athletes can compete with each other to see who can stay in for the longest period of time without making a mistake.

From Karl Rohnke, *Funn Stuff I* (Kendall/Hunt Publishing: Dubuque, Iowa, 1996).

Championship-Level Environment

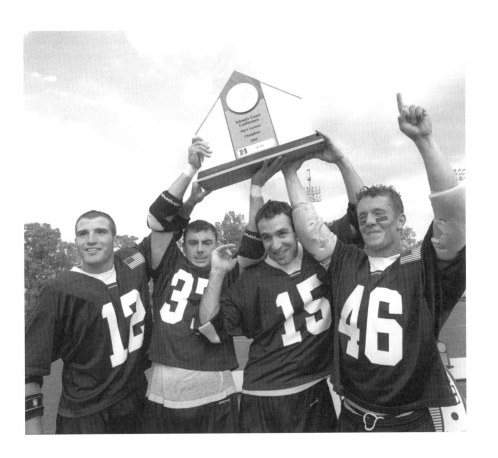

TEAM RETREATS

GOAL
Provide an opportunity for athletes to spend time with fellow teammates and coaches in a setting away from campus.

NUMBERS
No limit.

EQUIPMENT
Athletes might be required to bring linens and towels, depending on where you go.

SPACE
Preferably a self-contained site where athletes can all stay together.

SAFETY
Follow all rules as stipulated by the owners/managers of the facility.

GAME PLAN
This is an excellent activity to be carried out during the preseason or off-season depending on any rules stipulated by the governing bodies at your level. It is important to locate a site that is away from your normal training facility, where athletes can spend at least one night together. If you have a smaller team, it is ideal to have everyone stay in the same house or facility. If you have a larger team, it is ideal to stay at a camp or retreat site that is self-contained and where athletes can stay in close proximity to each other. It is best to avoid staying in a hotel if at all possible as most teams stay in hotels when they travel. This should be something different or "special" for your team. You can plan practice time while you are there if a facility is available. However, it is best to also allow for substantial "down time" for your athletes while they are on this retreat so they can be with each other in a relaxed atmosphere. Allow athletes to play board games, cards or whatever else they view as fun and relaxing (as long as it is appropriate, of course). Athletes can also work together to cook meals. This form of teamwork can be accomplished by assigning particular groups to various tasks such as setting the table, preparing the meals and cleaning afterwards. These tasks can be assigned on a rotating basis, depending on how many meals are served. You can also arrange for athletes to participate in other planned activities such as skits, or other fun, interactive games such as those described in this book. It is important to keep in mind that the goal of a retreat is for your athletes to have fun and have a chance to learn more about their teammates and coaches in a novel environment.

WRAP-UP
Did you learn anything new about any of your teammates or coaches?
What was it like to prepare the meals together?
How can this time together benefit our team?

VARIATIONS
Allow coaches to participate in most if not all of the activities with athletes during the retreat.
Give the leaders or captains of the team a great deal of responsibility in organizing activities once at the site.

TEAM *JEOPARDY*

GOAL
Give members of your team and staff an opportunity to get to know more about each other.

NUMBERS
No limit.

EQUIPMENT
A grid you design with enough boxes to write a blurb about each member of the team and staff. For example, if there are 25 athletes, then use a 5 x 5 grid.

SPACE
Locker room, classroom or any other space where athletes will not be disturbed.

SAFETY
N/A.

GAME PLAN
Begin this activity by designing a grid on a sheet of paper with enough boxes for each member of the team to have one. You can include the staff in this as well. Once you have designed the grid, ask each member of the team and staff to submit a blurb. These blurbs should be information that the team might find interesting about him or information he would like for the team to know about him. The information does not have to be personal. At the beginning of the month, give each person a copy of the grid. You can give it to them as a hard copy or send it as an e-mail attachment. Over the course of the month, team members and staff have the opportunity to do some sleuthing to determine who wrote each blurb. At month's end, have a verbal disclosure where you allow the team to look at the grid together and guess the person who is described in each square. Each person reveals his identity, and inevitably there will be stories behind each blurb. Have a small prize for the person who is able to guess most accurately. Asking for multiple blurbs will provide months of material, so you can do this activity several times.

WRAP-UP
At some point in the season, ask your athletes how they enjoyed this activity. Did it help you get to know your teammates and coaches better?
Why is it important to know about teammates outside sport?
How does this help our team accomplish our goals?

VARIATIONS
Use favorite quotes instead of blurbs in each square.
Establish a trophy or other symbol of the team that can go to the person who guessed most accurately. Each person has possession of the trophy for one month.

Contributed by Shelley Johnson, Assistant Coach, University of North Carolina Field Hockey.

SKIT NIGHT

GOAL
Reinforce the importance of teamwork, camaraderie and being able to step outside one's comfort zone while having fun.

NUMBERS
No limit.

EQUIPMENT
None.

SPACE
Any area where athletes can conduct their skit without obstructions.

SAFETY
Remind athletes to avoid any dangerous stunts that may cause injury.

GAME PLAN
This activity can occur at any point during the year, but is probably most effective at the beginning of the season when athletes are still getting to know each other. Begin this activity by deciding on a theme for skit night. For example, teams have used themes such as Hawaiian Luau, Night at the Cotton Club (famous nightclub in the 1920s), the *Andy Griffith Show,* etc. You can certainly get feedback from your captains on themes that would be most appropriate for your team. Once you have arrived at a theme, divide the team into smaller subunits by position or class and instruct them that they will have two days to develop a skit they will act out. Sit back and watch the creativity and fun your team will have with this activity.

WRAP-UP
Did any of you feel silly acting your part in front of your teammates and coaches?
Were you able to laugh at yourself and have fun?
Why is it important to be able to move beyond your "comfort zone"?
Are there times you might have to do that on our team?

VARIATIONS
Allow subunits or teams of classmates to arrive at their own theme rather than giving them one ahead of time.

TEAM CULTURE DEBATE

GOAL
Provide teammates an opportunity to learn more about each other and differing views on components of a healthy team culture.

NUMBERS
No limit.

EQUIPMENT
N/A

SPACE
Any open space large enough for team members to move around freely.

SAFETY
It is important that teammates are respectful of other opinions. A climate of healthy debate should be established at the beginning of the activity.

GAME PLAN
Begin the activity by informing team members they will be participating in a friendly debate and they have three options to choose from as they respond to statements you make. The responses are agree, disagree or undecided. Inform them that they will be required to physically move to a designated section of the room based on their choice of responses (e.g., agree to the right, disagree to the left and undecided in the middle). Statements you choose should be applicable to the gender and age make-up of your team. To stimulate discussion, you might begin with statements about pop culture or current events in the world. Allow ample time for discussion of each statement before moving to the next statement. Individuals are allowed to change sides once they hear arguments from the opposing view. Sample statements that have been used with teams before include the following.

- Angelina Jolie is a positive role model for young women in this country.
- Barry Bonds should have an asterisk by his name in the record book.
- Corporate sponsors should drop Tiger Woods as a representative of their products.
- In order for a team to be successful, it is important that teammates like each other.
- Conflict on a team is healthy. (Do not define conflict for them)
- Drinking in moderation during the season is okay. (Do not provide your definition of moderation)
- Everyone on this team is fully committed to helping this team be successful.
- In its current state, this team functions as a highly effective team.

WRAP-UP
This activity should create a great deal of discussion and team members will have fun with it.

What was it like when someone disagreed with you?
Why is it important to respect differing opinions on certain issues?
Why is it important that we all agree on certain issues?

COMMITMENT CONTRACT

GOAL
Gain a meaningful commitment from team members on essential components of team success.

NUMBERS
No limit.

EQUIPMENT
Chalkboard, easel or other space to write on where the entire group can see it.
Small poster board to be laminated.
Smaller laminated papers to be placed in individual lockers.

SPACE
Locker room, classroom or any space where athletes will not be disturbed.

SAFETY
N/A.

GAME PLAN
This is an activity that should be done during preseason. Begin this process by having athletes form subunits or small groups and brainstorm four or five essential components of team success. Have someone from each group share the results of their discussions with the entire group. Someone should record these where everyone can see them. Once athletes have arrived at an exhaustive list, allow members of the coaching staff to provide their input on components they feel are vital. Once this is done, everyone should decide on five or six essential components they can all commit to as a team. After establishing the components that everyone feels are essential, it is important to gain a commitment from everyone involved, including team managers and other support staff if appropriate.

Devise a contract based on the components the team thinks are important. That contract should include specific behaviors that relate to the essential components. For example, if a professional work ethic is an essential component of success, a specific behavior would be athletes committing to having a purpose for every single practice. You should have each athlete, coach, staff member and member of the support staff sign this contract. Laminate it, and post it somewhere that everyone can see it on a regular basis. Make smaller copies for everyone to place in their lockers or dressing area. It is important for the team to revisit this contract on a regular basis throughout the year to determine if the commitment level is where it should be for everyone.

WRAP-UP
Was this exercise effective in helping you and the team focus on the essential components of success?

WHO ARE THE PEOPLE IN OUR NEIGHBORHOOD?

GOAL
Help athletes realize and respect the contributions of support staff for the team.

NUMBERS
No limit.

EQUIPMENT
Digital camera.

SPACE
Location where you can show pictures of support staff as a slide presentation.

SAFETY
N/A.

GAME PLAN
Many times athletes have little knowledge and/or appreciation of the amount of work that people behind the scenes do to make things happen. This is an excellent activity to help your athletes realize the impact of the "anonymous and unseen" support staff of the program. Begin this activity by using a digital camera to take pictures of "the people that you meet when you're walking down the street," such as the associate athletic director, the secretaries, the training staff, the strength and conditioning staff, the equipment managers, the cleaning staff, the grounds crew, the event management staff, academic support, finance office, travel office, etc. The athletes should be able to put a name to a face for these people, and they should have an understanding of how these people help the program run. Once you have pictures of all of these people, put them into a Power Point slide show. For those of you who are "technologically challenged," you can elicit the help of your audiovisual person. Show the pictures during a team meeting and provide the names and a short background on each support staff person. In the end, athletes will know a little more about these very important people and hopefully can address them by name and thank them for the work.

WRAP-UP
How many of you realized how many people it takes to run our program?
What can you do in the next few weeks to show your appreciation to these people?

VARIATIONS
You can have your captains or other athletes take the pictures and conduct the slide presentation.

Contributed by Shelley Johnson, Assistant Coach, University of North Carolina Field Hockey.

Maintaining a Good Balance

GOAL
Reinforce the importance of balancing all aspects of an athlete's life, as well as encourage problem solving, cooperation, leadership and trust among teammates.

NUMBERS
8-16 is ideal. Consider dividing team into smaller subunits if more than 16.

EQUIPMENT
One 2" x 6" board, 7 feet long, for each team or subunit.
One 2" x 4" fulcrum attached to the middle of each of the 2" x 6" boards to make it a balancing board.
One segment of rope that is 20 feet long or longer for each team or subunit.
String or rope to be used for a boundary.

SAFETY
Ensure each team or subunit is always in contact with the ground or board to prevent anyone from jumping.

GAME PLAN
Have the team stand behind a boundary that is 12"-18" from the end of the balance board. The goal of the activity is for the entire team to cross the board without letting it touch the ground at either end. If the board does touch the ground, the group must start over from the beginning. Team members must always be in contact with the ground or the board.

WRAP-UP
What was necessary to get the team across?
How well did you plan?

VARIATION
Have the team split in half and switch sides.

Karl Rohnke, Silver Bullets (Project Adventure, Inc.: Beverly, MA, 1984).

ROLE APPRECIATION CARDS

GOAL
Help athletes appreciate their roles and those of their teammates.

NUMBERS
No limit.

EQUIPMENT
Enough note cards for each athlete to write something about each of her teammates (e.g., 10 athletes on a team will require 90 cards).

SPACE
Locker room, classroom or any space where athletes will not be disturbed.

SAFETY
N/A.

GAME PLAN
Give every member of the team a note card for each of the other team members. Once everyone has enough note cards, instruct athletes to write the name of one of their teammates on each card. Then she is required to provide several positive characteristics about that teammate on her respective card. For example, she can write about the role of that particular athlete on the team, what makes her unique, what she brings to the team that no one else does, what makes her a great teammate, etc. At the completion of this activity, each athlete will have a collection of affirmations from her teammates regarding her role on the team. The note cards help each player define her role on the team and realize its importance—however large or small, obvious or subtle it may be. She will more likely realize she isn't "toiling away" unnoticed, and that her role is appreciated. As a result, if she understands her role and knows it is appreciated, she will likely be more willing to accept it. Encourage your athletes to keep these cards somewhere they can see them on a regular basis. In reality, they will be likely to keep these cards long after they finish playing on your team.

WRAP-UP
How does it feel to see how your teammates appreciate you and the role you play on this team?
How can we continually appreciate every role on our team?

VARIATIONS
Before team members hear from each other, athletes can perform a preliminary activity. It is a simple writing exercise that requires them to actively identify and articulate their perception of their own roles on the team. She should begin every sentence with the phrase, "I am the player who..." This will encourage stream of consciousness and get ideas flowing. Each athlete will be responsible for identifying her role and teammates would be responsible for expressing an appreciation for it. In turn, this will increase the likelihood of each athlete accepting her role.

Contributed by Shelley Johnson, Assistant Coach, University of North Carolina Field Hockey.

CHANGING ROLES

GOAL
Help athletes develop an appreciation for the roles their teammates play on the team.

NUMBERS
No limit.

EQUIPMENT
None.

SPACE
N/A.

SAFETY
Make sure athletes can safely participate in the sport in a different role than they assume during practice.

GAME PLAN
Sometimes athletes have little appreciation for other roles on a team because all of their focus is on their own plight and whether or not they are being treated fairly or adequately appreciated. This is an excellent activity to provide all athletes on your team with an appreciation for their teammates and the roles they play to help the team be successful. At some point (preferably during pre-season) have your athletes switch positions with someone else on the team during drills or a scrimmage. For example in basketball, have your post players play guard and vice versa. In baseball, have your pitchers play catcher and your catchers go to the mound and pitch. It will not take them long to have a better understanding of what it takes to play different positions.

WRAP-UP
What was it like to play a different position?
What surprised you most about playing that position?
How might you view that position differently after playing it?
Why is it important that we appreciate the roles our teammates play on this team?

From Jeff Janssen, *Championship Team Building: What Every Coach Needs to Know to Build a Motivated, Committed and Cohesive Team* (Winning the Mental Game: Cary, North Carolina, 2002).

COMMITMENT CARDS

GOAL
Reinforce the importance of accountability and trust among teammates.

NUMBERS
No limit. Consider dividing team into smaller subunits if larger than 20.

EQUIPMENT
Index cards.

SPACE
Locker room, classroom or any space where athletes will not be disturbed.

SAFETY
N/A.

GAME PLAN
This activity encourages athletes to think about what they want to achieve in several aspects of their lives, such as sport, school, family, friends and volunteer work. They will also be required to think about how they can systematically go about achieving it. Once a month or however often you determine is appropriate, schedule a team meeting where each athlete on the team is required to read a commitment card aloud to her teammates. The "commitment card" specifies an area of her life she wants to improve. As each athlete reads her card aloud in front of the team, she is making a commitment to the team to accomplish this goal. In turn, one of her teammates volunteers to help her in pursuit of this goal. This is a selfless act on the part of the teammate. The energy and investment of two, rather than one, go a long way to help each athlete achieve her goal. The second teammate signs her card, and the card is posted on the first teammate's locker as a declaration of commitment and reminder. You will find that athletes will volunteer to help in different ways depending on the nature of the goal and their ability to contribute.

WRAP-UP
Periodically ask your athletes how they like this activity.
How does it help with accountability and trust among your teammates?

Contributed by Shelley Johnson, Assistant Coach, University of North Carolina Field Hockey

TEAM COUNCIL MEETING

GOAL
To provide athletes and coaches an opportunity to discuss various aspects of the team environment.

NUMBERS
At least one athlete representing each class in school or position on the team.

EQUIPMENT
None.

SPACE
Locker room, classroom or any space where you will not be disturbed.

SAFETY
Provide an environment where athletes feel they can voice their opinions about the team culture.

GAME PLAN
Coaches often spend the majority of their time in game preparation and comparatively little time soliciting feedback from their athletes regarding the environment on the team. This activity is an excellent way to stay in touch with your athletes and the team environment. Begin by allowing athletes to elect teammates that will serve as team representatives to the coaching staff. Depending on the type of team you coach, these representatives might come from each class in school (e.g., sophomore, junior) or each position on the team (e.g., defensive secondary in football, distance runner in track and field). For maximum effectiveness, limit the number of athletes to 12 or fewer. Once representatives are elected, establish a regular meeting time (at least twice a month) where coaches and athletes can meet to discuss current issues related to team success. These meetings should take place somewhere other than a coach's office so athletes feel more comfortable relaying their concerns and ideas. Allow athletes to provide the coaching staff with feedback on aspects of the team that are going well, and aspects they feel can be improved to increase the likelihood of success. Coaches should also be allowed to provide athletes feedback regarding issues they deem important. Athletes *and* coaches must remember that this time is not a gripe session or an environment to air dirty laundry. Rather it is a time to keep both groups informed of the current status of the team. The ability of athletes and coaches to refrain from being defensive will be a key to the success of this process.

WRAP-UP
Are these meetings effective?
Do you feel you are able to be completely honest during these meetings?
What can we do to improve this process?
Do you think we should continue to conduct these meetings?

VARIATIONS
Allow every member of the team to participate in the meetings if the team is small enough.

OUR TEAM IS LIKE A HAND

GOAL
Help athletes see the similarities of the working parts of a team with the fingers on a person's hand.

NUMBERS
No limit.

EQUIPMENT
None.

SPACE
Any available space

SAFETY
N/A.

GAME PLAN
This activity will reinforce the importance of individuals on a team working together. Begin this activity by showing athletes your hand, or encourage them to look at one of their own hands. Explain to them that a cohesive team is like a person's hand. To function well, a hand needs all four fingers and a thumb. Using each finger you can make an analogy to the way you feel the team should function and how teammates should treat each other. Show them your little finger first. Ask team members what they see and think of as you hold your little finger out by itself away from the rest of the fingers. By itself, it is vulnerable and is often injured. It needs the other fingers to provide stability. And it is also a vital finger because very few skills in any sport can be accomplished without the little finger. This is an appropriate analogy for the smaller or less visible roles on the team and their importance to the overall success of the team. Show them the ring finger next and ask them to think about what the ring on a finger means. This will provide an excellent opportunity to discuss the importance of everyone's total commitment to the team's goals and vision. Show them the middle finger next. You will almost certainly get laughter or snickering from your athletes, but remind them that this finger represents put-downs and disrespect for others. Showing this finger will serve as an important reminder that your team cannot afford put-downs and disrespect among teammates. There must be a sense of respect and appreciation for everyone on the team. Show your team your index finger by pointing somewhere out in front of you. This is a symbol that your team must always be focused on where it is going. It is important to learn from the past, but vital that the team always has a vision and is continually moving forward and improving. Show them your thumb with a "thumbs-up." This can represent the importance of teammates encouraging each other and an overall positive environment on the team.

WRAP-UP
Can you see how the hand is similar to the components of a successful team? What will each of you do to make sure "our hand" is strong?

THESE SHOES WERE MADE FOR TALKING

GOAL
Encourage athletes to examine the everyday team culture.

NUMBERS
No limit.

EQUIPMENT
Various pieces of equipment from your sport.

SPACE
Locker room, playing or practice surface or classroom.

SAFETY
N/A.

GAME PLAN
It is important to have athletes occasionally examine the team culture. One way to do this is to discuss it during team meetings. An effective strategy for doing this is to ask athletes, "If your shoes could talk, what would they say about how we do things around here?" or "If your shoes could talk, would they say we have a championship environment in every aspect of our program?" The great thing about referring to the shoes the athletes wear is that their shoes go everywhere with them when they are involved in the sport. They are able to "see" everything that goes on in the environment.

FOLLOW-UP
Are all of you doing your part to develop and maintain a championship atmosphere on our team?

Are there specific things we need to do differently as a team to enhance the culture on our team?

VARIATIONS
Different pieces of equipment from your sport (e.g., shoes, sticks, balls, bags) could be used instead of the athletes' shoes.

As with the **Team Symbol** activity in this book (see next page), athletes could choose a piece of equipment that best represents their part in the championship-level environment. Examples of equipment that have been chosen include: a mouth guard for the communicator, a shoe for the fastest team member, a stick for the goal scorer, a sweatband for the athlete who works the hardest, a pair of Spandex for the one who dives for loose balls (Spandex protects the skin from turf or floor burns), etc.

TEAM SYMBOL

GOAL
Encourage athletes to reflect on how they see the team, as well as how they see their own roles on the team.

NUMBERS
No limit. Consider dividing team into smaller subunits if more than 30 athletes.

EQUIPMENT
None.

SPACE
Locker room, playing or practice surface or classroom.

SAFETY
N/A.

GAME PLAN
Have each athlete find something he feels represents the team, as well as something that represents his role on the team. Give your athletes several days to find these symbols. Remind athletes that their individual symbols should reflect how they view their role on the larger team. Bring the team together and have each athlete share the symbol he feels best represents the team and the symbol that best represents his role within that team. If possible, have the athletes keep these symbols in their lockers or anywhere they can be seen on a regular basis.

WRAP-UP
Why did you pick the symbol you picked?
Did any of the symbols surprise or inspire you?
How can we use these symbols throughout the year?

VARIATIONS
Have athletes vote on one symbol that best represents the team and then have T-shirts made with a picture of the team symbol on them. The University of Michigan Field Hockey team did this in 2002 when they won the national championship. The team had shirts made where the front read "Be the Boat." The back of the shirt had a picture of a ski boat. The idea for this shirt originated from an analogy presented by one of the team members: You can be the boat or you can be the skier being pulled behind the boat. You can lead or you can follow. You can be the captain of your own destiny or allow others to dictate your fate. Michigan chose to be the boat.

Athletes can also write the team symbol on their shoes or some piece of equipment to serve as a constant reminder during competition.

Contributed by Stephanie Johnson, former field hockey player, University of Michigan.

BIG BROTHER/BIG SISTER PROGRAM

GOAL
Foster communication and trust between experienced and less-experienced athletes.

NUMBERS
No limit.

EQUIPMENT
None.

SPACE
N/A.

SAFETY
N/A.

GAME PLAN
Occasionally a team can experience an undesirable division between athletes who have been a part of the program for a while and newer athletes. One way to alleviate this is to assign experienced athletes to less-experienced athletes to serve as mentors. This can be accomplished by randomly assigning an experienced athlete to each of the new athletes, or they can be allowed to pick the athlete they would like to mentor. Once mentors are assigned, they can assist the new athletes in several ways, such as helping them register for classes, learn their way around campus, move into the dorm, etc. They can also schedule regular times to eat meals together or other social events. The idea is that the less-experienced athlete feels a connection with at least one of the more experienced athletes.

WRAP-UP
How did you like this experience as a new athlete to our program?
How did you like serving as a mentor?
Should we continue this activity?

Notes from Coach

GOAL
Let athletes know you believe in them and appreciate their efforts.

NUMBERS
No limit.

EQUIPMENT
Note cards.

SPACE
N/A.

SAFETY
N/A.

GAME PLAN
This activity will take a little effort on your part, but the effort will be worthwhile in many ways. Athletes appreciate it when their coach recognizes them for a job well done in practice or gives them a vote of confidence before competition. One very effective way to communicate with your athletes is by writing notes to them. These notes do not have to be elaborate or eloquent. But they will provide something tangible that your athletes can carry with them long after they are written. One college lacrosse coach wrote a note to one of his players that said, "If I were nineteen years old again, you and I would be best friends. That is how much I appreciate and respect you as person and as a player." He then put the note in the athlete's locker. A middle-school basketball coach bought note cards that said, "Believe in Yourself." She then wrote a personal note to each of her players on the cards indicating how much she appreciated their efforts and how proud she was of them. She then placed a note in each athlete's locker before a tournament game.

WRAP-UP
You don't really have to ask follow-up questions about this activity. You can be assured your athletes will appreciate your willingness to take the time to write personal notes.

Contributed by Paula Farrell, Athletic Director and Coach, Harford Day School, Bel Air, Maryland.

ESTABLISHING A CULTURE OF "TOUGHNESS"

GOAL
Begin to establish a culture of "toughness" on your team.

NUMBERS
No limit.

EQUIPMENT
Forms that contain questions you have written.
Pencils or pens.

SPACE
Locker room, classroom or any space where athletes will not be disturbed.

SAFETY
N/A.

GAME PLAN
This is an excellent activity if your team does not handle adversity very effectively or is easily distracted by external factors. Begin the activity by having the entire team define *team* toughness and *individual* toughness. Once they have had an opportunity to discuss these two, you can write a series of questions your athletes will answer. They will answer two sets of questions in this activity. One set of questions targets toughness as a team and the other set of questions targets individual toughness. The following questions are suggestions for the team. Which team is the toughest you have ever played against during your career? What made this team so tough in your mind? What would our opponents say about the toughness of *our* team? What do we need to do to become a tougher team? Possible questions concerning individual toughness might include the following. Who is the toughest athlete you have ever competed against during your career? What made this athlete so tough? What would your teammates and opponents say about *your* toughness? What do *you* need to do to increase *your* toughness as an athlete? Once the activity is finished, it is important to follow up with indivitual and team goal-setting that targets areas in need of improvement.

WRAP-UP
What did you learn about yourself and this team?
Are there specific strategies you and this team can use to increase our toughness?

VARIATIONS
Use this same format for any specific type of culture you are attempting to develop on your team.

Contributed by Kerstin Kimel, Head Coach, Duke University Women's Lacrosse.

ROLE-PLAY DEALING WITH ADVERSITY

GOAL
Help athletes realize the different ways to respond to adversity.

NUMBERS
No limit.

EQUIPMENT
None.

SPACE
Locker room, classroom or on the practice or playing surface.

SAFETY
N/A.

GAME PLAN
Team members should be divided into small groups or units. The number in each group depends on the size of your team. The ideal situation would be to have athletes divide into subunits that currently exist on your team. Provide each unit with a scenario that might cause individuals or the entire unit to become frustrated. Examples might be poor officiating, adverse weather conditions, an athlete not playing his or her role effectively, the team losing by a large margin, etc. The key is to provide scenarios that team members might have a difficult time handling or have not handled well in the past. Once given the scenarios, each group should then spend 5-7 minutes devising a plan to role-play an inappropriate or "mentally weak" response to the adversity and then role-play a more appropriate, "mentally tough" response. Athletes will have a good time with this exercise, but will become more aware of how they appear to others when not handling adversity in a proper manner. They will also be more aware of the importance of responding more appropriately to adversity.

WRAP-UP
What was your experience during this activity?
What do you think of the different types of responses?
What can you and/or your teammates do to ensure a more appropriate response to adversity in the future?
How can you practice more appropriate responses in practice?

From Jeff Janssen, *Championship Team Building: What Every Coach Needs to Know to Build a Motivated, Committed and Cohesive Team* (Winning the Mental Game: Cary, North Carolina, 2002).

WHAT MY COACH CAN DO TO MOTIVATE ME

GOAL
Allow more insight into what motivates the various athletes on your team.

NUMBERS
No limit.

SPACE
Your office.

SAFETY
Provide an environment where your athletes are willing to discuss what motivates them.

GAME PLAN
As a coach, you spend countless hours with your athletes in practice and preparation for competition. Because you spend all of this time attempting to help your athletes peak at the right time and perform to their potential each time they compete, it seems obvious that it is important to know "what buttons to push" when trying to motivate your athletes and help them stay focused. What better way to accomplish this than to ask them? Too often, coaches assume they know how to motivate their athletes or they assume that athletes are all motivated by the same tactics. In reality, it is rare when every athlete on a team will respond to the same motivational tactics from their coach. This activity provides you an opportunity to take the guesswork out of what you should say to your athletes when they are competing. You should arrange individual meetings with each of your athletes and ask them, "When it is game time or when it is time to compete, what can I do as a coach to help you perform at your best?" If you have a large team and several assistants, it is important for assistants to conduct this activity with each of the athletes they directly coach on a daily basis. If the coaching staff has created an atmosphere where athletes feel free to discuss what works best for them, all of you will have much greater insight and will be more effective coaches.

WRAP-UP
You can ask questions regarding this activity at the end of the season as a part of the overall evaluation of your program. You can ask questions similar to the following:

What did you think of your coaches asking for your input on how to best motivate you?

Was it effective?

Should we continue to do it?

How can we improve on the process of conducting this activity?

VARIATIONS
Conduct the individual meetings somewhere other than your office. This will allow your athletes to feel more comfortable discussing how to best motivate them.

WHAT MY TEAMMATES CAN DO TO MOTIVATE ME

GOAL

Allow athletes to tell their teammates the most effective ways to motivate them when they are struggling.

NUMBERS

No limit. Consider dividing team into smaller subunits if you have a large team. It is especially effective to divide team into subunits by position or event.

SPACE

Any space athletes will not be disturbed.

SAFETY

N/A.

GAME PLAN

Begin this activity by explaining that all athletes are motivated in different ways. For example, some athletes respond better when teammates "get in their faces" and verbally challenge them, while others respond better when a teammate encourages them. As a team it is important that each athlete is aware of what his teammates need from him when they are struggling with their confidence or even when they are not putting forth maximum effort. Tell athletes to take a minute or two to reflect upon what their teammates can do to help them in these types of situations. Then have each athlete verbalize this information to his teammates. Even if you have a medium-sized team (15-20 athletes), it might be more effective to divide the team into subunits by position. The reality is that athletes cannot always say the right things. But they will have a better understanding of what to say and how to encourage their teammates after participating in this activity.

WRAP-UP

Did you learn anything new about any of your teammates?
Why is it important to know what motivates your teammates?
What will you do to remember what you have learned about your teammates?

ATHLETES PLANNING AND CONDUCTING PRACTICE

GOAL
Allow athletes to develop leadership skills and provide ownership of practice.

NUMBERS
No limit.

EQUIPMENT
None.

SPACE
Activity will take place at practice.

SAFETY
All drills and activities should have your final approval before being implemented in practice.

GAME PLAN
Provide your captains an opportunity to practice their leadership skills by allowing them to plan and lead one aspect of practice. This opportunity will help them develop as leaders and will give you an idea of how the team responds to them. You might be surprised, but these drills or aspects of practice will most likely be some of the most energetic and effective that are run all year. The captains will have ownership and will feel a level of accountability.

WRAP-UP
How did you like that drill?
Why was it effective or ineffective?

VARIATIONS
Allow other members of your team to plan and lead one part of practice.
Allow captains to lead larger portions of practice and eventually an entire practice based on their ability to effectively lead.

ALTER EGO

GOAL
Encourage and allow athletes to take on a different persona and free themselves to compete.

NUMBERS
No limit.

EQUIPMENT
None.

SPACE
Any space.

SAFETY
N/A.

GAME PLAN
Some athletes have a difficult time making the transition from their non-competitive personality away from sport and the persona needed to perform at a high level in sport. Certainly athletes can and should commit to work harder in the weight room or in conditioning drills to help them become "tougher" or to develop a more competitive persona. And, as the coach it is important for you to create more competitive situations in practice to encourage this mentality. However, you still might have athletes who will not allow themselves to make that transition to being more competitive.

One activity that is effective in helping athletes make this transition is to encourage them to take on a different persona or even "become a different person" when they compete. You can begin this process by asking the entire team to discuss what it means to be tough or to play without worrying about making mistakes. The areas you choose to focus will depend on what you feel your team or individuals on your team need to improve upon. For example, some athletes need to improve on their ability to challenge each other by being more competitive in practice and not holding grudges once practice is finished. As athletes begin to discuss these characteristics, you should ask those athletes who do make a successful transition into the competitive mode to describe how they accomplish it. As other athletes listen, they will begin to see how they might make that transition.

Instruct team members that they can take some time to think of ways they will more effectively make the transition. Inform athletes that one option they can utilize is to decide upon an alter ego or different personality they would like to become as they prepare to compete. This persona can be of a fictional character, or another athlete that personifies what this athlete wants to be like. Athletes might also name this other persona to help personalize it and bring it to life. Bring the team back together after a few days and allow each team member to share the name they have given their alter ego and how this will help them be more competitive.

WRAP-UP
Why is it important to make the transition to the "athlete" mode?

What will be the most challenging aspect of this process for you?

If you aren't choosing an alter ego, what is your plan to help make the transition that you need you to make?

ATHLETES RESPONSIBLE FOR SCOUTING REPORT

GOAL
Encourage accountability and develop leadership among team members.

NUMBERS
No limit.

EQUIPMENT
None.

SPACE
N/A.

SAFETY
N/A.

GAME PLAN
This activity involves allowing at least one of your athletes to take responsibility for portions of the scouting report for each opponent you play during the season. You can begin the process by having your captains or team leaders serve as the first to take on this responsibility. Athletes that are involved in this process will become better students of the game as a result of watching game film with coaches, devising portions of the game plan and presenting it to the entire team. All of this would be under the supervision of a coach.

WRAP-UP
Get feedback from your athletes throughout the season on how this process works.

Contributed by Duke University Women's Basketball.

ATHLETES PROVIDING EACH OTHER WITH FEEDBACK

GOAL
Allow athletes the opportunity to see how their teammates view them in relation to various situations with the team.

NUMBERS
No limit.

EQUIPMENT
Forms that contain questions you have written.
Pencils or pens.

SPACE
Locker room, classroom or any space where athletes will not be disturbed.

SAFETY
N/A.

GAME PLAN
This is a great activity to get members of your team to provide their teammates with feedback regarding their confidence in each other in various situations. Many times coaches indicate they would like to create an environment where athletes can be honest with each other on issues that affect the team. This activity is a very effective way to begin to establish that culture, because athletes will be getting honest feedback from their teammates in an anonymous fashion. To begin this activity you should write a series of questions you feel are relevant to the success of your team. For example, you can ask questions such as the following: "Other than yourself, which of your teammates do you want to take the last shot in a game?" "Which of your teammates do you feel is the best leader on this team?" "Which of your teammates has the best work ethic in practice?" "Which of your teammates best exemplifies a 'team player'?" "Which of your teammates is the most committed to the team's mission?" "Who has made the greatest commitment to improve?"

Once you have composed your list of questions, give it to your athletes and ask them to rank each of their teammates on each question. The first athlete they list is the one that best exemplifies that quality. You will then need to compile the answers and conduct a composite ranking on each question. Then give this information back to your athletes. At this point it is imperative to stress that each athlete will have a choice in how he responds to the feedback his teammates are providing him. It is important for athletes to look at this information as a challenge and begin to make a commitment to improve any areas in which they were ranked lower than they expected. They should feel good about areas where they are ranked highly and continue what they have been doing. This activity will help your athletes gain a realistic perspective on how their teammates view them. Some of them will be surprised they were ranked so highly and some will realize their teammates want them to work harder in some areas. Regardless, your team will be on its way to providing honest feedback with each other.

WRAP-UP
How did you like this activity?
Was it difficult to see how your teammates ranked you?
Why is it important for us to be honest with each other on this team?
What should you do if someone provides you with honest feedback that you don't necessarily agree with?

ATHLETES EVALUATING YOUR PROGRAM

GOAL
Provide more insight into how your athletes view your program.

NUMBERS
No limit.

SPACE
Locker room, classroom or any space where athletes will not be disturbed.

SAFETY
Provide an environment where athletes can be honest in their evaluations.

GAME PLAN
As a coach or coaching staff, you are continually providing feedback to your athletes. They are often graded on a weekly or daily basis on their performance. How often do your athletes provide you with feedback regarding your coaching and how you run your program? Begin this activity by devising a simple form that includes specific aspects of your coaching as well as questions you feel address all aspects of your program. For example, you can have your athletes rate you on specific aspects of coaching such as knowledge of the sport, organization of practice, game coaching, respect of the players, ability to teach skills, pride in your work, ability to communicate effectively, willingness to listen, consistency in areas such as discipline of athletes and your disposition on a daily basis, etc. Examples of questions you might ask include the following. "What are my strongest points as a coach?" "What areas do I need to improve most in as a coach?" "Was I fair to all of the athletes on this team? If not, why?" "Are there specific areas of our program that could be improved such as the way we run practice, pre-game activities, post-game activities, etc.?" Athletes should be allowed to provide feedback on each coach they interact with on a regular basis. Athletes should be allowed to provide this feedback anonymously to encourage honest feedback. Finally, this exercise will only be effective if you are willing to objectively review the feedback you are given and to make changes in areas that are consistently regarded as needing improvement.

WRAP-UP
At some point, ask the leaders on your team if this exercise was beneficial and whether they want to continue it. Their response will most likely be determined by your willingness to use the information to make changes in your coaching and the overall program.

VARIATIONS
Ask your captains or leaders on the team to provide input on the types of questions and the areas that are covered on the evaluation form.

Trust

You Can Count on Me

GOAL
Highlight the importance of athletes trusting their teammates.

NUMBERS
No limit.

EQUIPMENT
None.

SPACE
Area that is level and free of any obstacles.

SAFETY
No horseplay.
Person falling must always be straight and rigid.

GAME PLAN
Begin this activity by having teammates get into pairs. Have one person stand with his back to his partner, with his arms straight out to the side, feet together and eyes closed. The athlete standing behind him must put his arms at a 45-degree angle under the arms of the first athlete. The athlete with his eyes closed should stand stiff with arms out and fall back. The athlete behind should catch his falling partner. The first couple of times this athlete should only fall about a foot. This can be repeated with a greater distance each time, but no more than 2 or 3 feet. Have the pair switch roles after a few times. You can also have team members find new partners.

WRAP-UP
Why do you think we did this activity?
How is trust involved in our sport and on our team?
What happens when teammates don't trust each other, both on and off the playing field?
What do we need to do to make sure we have an atmosphere where we can trust each other?

From Karl Rohnke, *Silver Bullets* (Project Adventure, Inc.: Beverly, MA, 1984).

LEAP OF FAITH

GOAL
Emphasize the importance of trust among teammates.

NUMBERS
At least 11.

EQUIPMENT
A stable platform to jump from, 2-4feet in height.

SPACE
Flat area free of obstacles.

SAFETY
No horseplay.
Remind athletes this is a more advanced trust activity and it must be taken seriously. Always lower the person diving gently to the ground.

GAME PLAN
This is a trust activity that is more advanced than the one-on-one trust fall; therefore, it probably should be a challenge by choice. To begin the activity, have a team member volunteer to stand on the jumping platform. The remainder of the team forms two lines shoulder to shoulder, facing each othe,r and put their hands out in front of them with palms up and elbows bent. The hands should look like a zipper, with the team members putting every other hand out, almost touching the stomach of the teammate across from them. The distance between the two lines should be about the width of the person diving. When the lines are ready, the jumper says, "jumping," and does not jump until the team says, "jump." The jumper dives up and out into the hands of teammates with arms extended, head up and landing at a slight angle. After the teammate is caught, the team must lower her to the ground feet-first.

WRAP-UP
What was it like to jump off the platform into the arms of your teammates?
Why do you think we did this activity?
How might this activity relate to our team?
What is the significance of trust to this team?

VARIATIONS
Allow athletes to start the activity by doing "Superman dives" into team members' arms. This is accomplished when an athlete takes a running start and leaps from the ground into their arms. This can be a good lead-up to diving from a platform above the ground.

From Karl Rohnke, *Silver Bullets* (Project Adventure, Inc.: Beverly, MA, 1984).

CAN I TRUST YOU?

GOAL
Help develop trust among team members.

NUMBERS
No limit, but at least two.

EQUIPMENT
Enough blindfolds for half of the group.
Traffic cones, chairs, balls and any other equipment you have at your disposal to create an obstacle course.

SPACE
Any space that is free of sharp or dangerous obstacles.

SAFETY
Athletes should be reminded to avoid running or purposely guiding someone into an obstacle.

GAME PLAN
Design an obstacle course that blindfolded athletes will have to negotiate while being verbally led by a sighted partner. The object is for the sighted partner to guide the blindfolded partner through a designated obstacle course without coming in contact with any of the obstacles. If a blindfolded athlete touches an obstacle, the pair must begin the course again.

WRAP-UP
What was that experience like for those of you who were blindfolded?
What was that experience like for those of you who were able to see?
Can you relate this experience to any situations that might occur on our team?

VARIATIONS
Create a more difficult obstacle course by having the athletes go up bleachers or steps. You can also have the athletes in a more natural setting outside. Being in the woods or other areas that might be perceived as more challenging will increase the need for trust between athletes.

From Karl Rohnke, Silver Bullets (Project Adventure, Inc.: Beverly, MA, 1984).

TRUSTING OUR LEADERS

GOAL
Provide an opportunity for athletes to take on leadership roles and emphasize the importance of communication and trust.

NUMBERS
8-15 is ideal. Consider dividing team into smaller subunits if more than 15.

EQUIPMENT
Blindfolds.

SPACE
Safe area where team members will not be injured.

SAFETY
Someone must spot athletes when going near or around dangerous obstacles. No horseplay.

GAME PLAN
Begin this activity by having the team pick two leaders, or you might assign the captains as leaders. You can use a variety of scenarios to set the tone for this activity. One way to set it up is to tell the team they are going on a journey together which could be the championship game or playoffs. Explain that any team which embarks on a journey must have strong leadership. Remind the team that there are always obstacles to be overcome in reaching a goal. In this exercise, one obstacle the team will have to overcome is that they will be blindfolded. A second obstacle to overcome is that they are not allowed to use normal means of communication. They can't talk. The leaders may talk, but are not allowed to touch the group members. Their journey will take them under, over, and around various barriers and obstacles. The blindfolded team members should be told to always remain in contact with each other. They can do this by forming a line. A second stipulation is that all blindfolded team members must be at the front of the line at least once during the course of the journey. Allow the team a planning period and encourage them to think of every obstacle that they might face and encourage them to prepare as they would prepare for a game. Take the team through doors, up stairs, between volleyball standards, under tables or around any other obstacle that can be difficult without posing the danger of injury.

WRAP-UP
Was it difficult to accomplish this task?
How important was it that the team put its trust in the leaders?

From Karl Rohnke, *Silver Bullets* (Project Adventure, Inc.: Beverly, MA, 1984).

I Can Carry You on My Back

GOAL
Help athletes realize their contributions and importance to the team.

NUMBERS
No limit. Consider dividing athletes into smaller subunits if more than 20.

EQUIPMENT
Sheet of paper, felt-tip marker and tape for each athlete.

SPACE
Locker room, classroom or playing or practice surface.

SAFETY
N/A.

GAME PLAN
Have each athlete put her name at the top of a sheet of paper. Athletes should then help each other so that every athlete has a piece of paper taped to her back. Athletes should then be instructed to go to each of the other athletes and write something that particular athlete contributes to team success. Once athletes have finished writing something for each member of the team, they can remove the paper and take a few minutes to read the comments. Have athletes place these sheets of paper somewhere they can see them on a regular basis as a reminder of what their teammates think of them and their contributions to the team.

WRAP-UP
What was it like to read what your teammates said about you?
Why is it important to do an activity like this one?
How else can we show teammates they are important to the team?

VARIATIONS
Athletes can write attributes they appreciate in their teammates.
Athletes can write behaviors or characteristics they expect from teammates.

MOUSE TRAP TRUST

GOAL
Learning to trust teammates and developing a willingness to take risks.

NUMBERS
No limit.

EQUIPMENT
One standard size mouse trap for each team member.
Enough blindfolds for half the team (optional).

SPACE
Gymnasium, carpeted floor or any surface that is flat where mouse traps can be placed without releasing.

SAFETY
It should be noted that we have conducted this activity on multiple occasions and it has never resulted in injury. The first safety rule is there should be no horse play. Take the time to teach the team members how to properly set the mouse traps. The traps should always be held on the opposite end from where the bait is placed. The snap bar should always be pulled toward the person setting the trap so that it won't pinch him if it releases unexpectedly. Once set, traps should always be held by placing fingers on both sides of the base.

GAME PLAN
Begin this activity by having team members get into pairs. One person should then be blindfolded. The sighted person should then set two traps and place them on the floor about shoulder width apart. The traps should be facing in the same direction. The blindfolded person should stand facing the traps with the bait end of the trap on the opposite side of where he is standing. He should then extend his arms out in front with palms flat, facing down so they are directly above the traps. The objective of the activity is for the sighted person to guide him so that he lowers his hands downward toward the traps. Once his hands are about two inches above the traps, he should be instructed to proceed to place his hands on top of the traps without setting them off. Once his hands are resting on the traps, he should hold this position for a few seconds and then remove his hands quickly to allow the traps to spring. Partners should switch roles and repeat the activity.

WRAP-UP
This is a great opportunity to discuss fear or failure and trust between teammates. You might ask questions such as the following:
Was it difficult to trust your partner? Why or why not?
Is trust important on our team? Why or why not?
What is the trust level on our team?

BALL OF STRING

GOAL
Encourage trust and accountability among teammates.

NUMBERS
No limit. Consider dividing athletes into smaller subunits if more than 10.

EQUIPMENT
One ball of string or small rope per subunit.

SPACE
Locker room, practice or playing surface or classroom.

SAFETY
N/A.

GAME PLAN
Begin this activity by having the team or subunit facing each other in a circle. One athlete begins the process by holding on to the end of the string and tossing the ball to another teammate. As he tosses the ball of string to the teammate he should indicate something that the team needs from that athlete for the team to be successful. The process continues until all athletes have been tossed the ball of string. At this point, have each athlete either lean back or take a step or two back while holding on to the string. The string will become very taut. After several seconds, take a pair of scissors and cut one or two portions of the string. By cutting the string, the taught web will be broken. This is a great representation of what might happen if one team member elects not do what his team needs from him for success.

WRAP-UP
What did it feel like when one of your teammates told everyone what was needed from you?

What happened when the team leaned back? What do you think that represented?

What was the significance of cutting the string?

How might that apply to what could happen on this team?

VARIATIONS
Once the activity is finished, have athletes cut small pieces of the string. Have athletes tie the piece of string to their equipment bag or place it somewhere they can see it often as a reminder of what the team needs from each of them. You can also put colored beads representing team colors on the string.

Communication

TEAM TELEPHONE

GOAL
Highlight how easily communication can break down on a team.

NUMBERS
No limit, but divide a large team into smaller subunits.

EQUIPMENT
None.

SPACE
Large enough space for athletes to stand in lines.

SAFETY
N/A.

GAME PLAN
This activity is similar to the old-fashioned "telephone game." The coach (or an athlete) begins by whispering a phrase into the ear of the first athlete. Each athlete in turn whispers the phrase to the person next to her. At the end of the line, the final athlete repeats out loud to the whole team what she has just heard. The team can be divided into two groups, given the same statement, and nearly always at the end the outcomes will differ. This will illustrate how it is everyone's responsibility on the team to listen, pay attention and communicate clearly and honestly (sometimes an athlete will change the phrase "just because") in order to achieve a goal or perform.

You can explain that listening and communication are skills that must be practiced and learned. In real situations, messages can be distorted from the coach to athletes, as well as athlete to athlete. As the coach, you can point out that there will be times when communication will break down and that misunderstandings, decreases in performance or conflicts may arise. This is normal. However, an effective team learns from it, and moves forward together. This exercise also illustrates that clarifying the understanding of the message is important—especially for you as the coach. A significant point for you to remember is that it is not what you actually say that is important—it is what the athlete hears and perceives.

WRAP-UP
Where did the communication start to break down in the chain?

Why did the communication start to break down in the chain?

What can each of you do to make sure there are no breakdowns in communication between you and your teammates?

What can you do to make sure you and the coaches avoid breakdowns in communication?

Contributed by Nicole Lavoi, Research and Program Associate for the Mendelson Center for Sports, Character and Community, University of Notre Dame.

The "Voice" of the Team

GOAL
Reinforce the importance of precise communication.

NUMBERS
No limit. Divide a large team into smaller subunits.

EQUIPMENT
Piece of paper and a pencil for each team member.
Person who is identified as the "voice" for each subunit is given a picture and a clipboard.

SPACE
Locker room, classroom or anyplace athletes will not be disturbed.

SAFETY
N/A.

GAME PLAN
Begin this activity by giving each team member a piece of paper and a pencil. Then assign one person to be the "voice of the team." Give this person a picture and a clipboard. This person is to put the picture on the clipboard so that none of the other team members can see it. The objective of this activity is for the "the voice" to describe the picture to the other team members so they can draw it on their pieces of paper. The "voice of the team" must describe the picture without using any hand signals. This person is not allowed to use shape terms such as circle, square, triangle, etc. in the description. Team members who are drawing are not allowed to ask any questions during this activity. You might start off with simple pictures of several lines through a particular shape (triangle, rectangle, etc.), then progress to more difficult drawings if athletes are able to communicate and draw those pictures easily.

WRAP-UP
What was difficult about that activity?
How did the communicators do in their descriptions?
What were the keys for those of you that were drawing the pictures?
How can we relate this to our team and the need for precise communication?

MINE FIELD

GOAL
Highlight the importance of communication and trust among teammates.

NUMBERS
16-20 is ideal. Consider dividing team into smaller subunits if more than 20.

EQUIPMENT
Blindfolds.
Numerous sports balls and other sports equipment or obstacles that are not dangerous to walk around when athletes are blindfolded.

SPACE
Flat area about a quarter the size of a basketball court.

SAFETY
Athletes should walk slowly with their hands in front for protection.

GAME PLAN
Before beginning this activity, you should mark an area with a rope, tape, or existing lines on a court about the size of a badminton court. The area can be larger depending on the size of your team. Spread the balls, equipment and obstacles throughout the area so it would be difficult for a blindfolded person to walk through the area without bumping his feet against an object. Once all objects are laid out on the floor, have the team members get into pairs. This is an opportune time for teammates that are having trouble getting along to be forced to work together. The object of this activity is for one teammate to verbally guide his teammate to the opposite end of the marked area, retrieve an object and return it to the starting spot without bumping into an object on the ground. Tell the athletes that the objects on the ground are like mines on a battlefield. The sighted people can be made to stay at the end of the marked area or can be free to walk around the outside of the area, but they are not allowed to touch their partners at any time. If a blindfolded athlete bumps into an object, he must go back to the start and begin again. All members of the team are participating in this activity at the same time. It forces the blindfolded athletes to focus on the commands of his or her partner and ignore the other people giving directions.

WRAP-UP
What were some of the problems you experienced during this activity?
Was it difficult to block out the noise and listen to your partner?
What did it take to reach your goal?
How can you relate this to being able to communicate with teammates in a noisy environment?

VARIATIONS
Mousetraps can be used as the obstacles to increase the intensity of the activity. It is important that athletes are wearing athletic shoes if mousetraps are used.

From Karl Rohnke, *The Bottomless Bag Again* (Kendall/Hunt Publishing, Dubuque, Iowa, 1994).

SQUEEZE PLAY

GOAL
Reinforce the importance of proper communication.

NUMBERS
12-25 people is ideal. Consider dividing team into smaller subunits if more than 25.

EQUIPMENT
One ball from your sport or a ball that represents a team's goal.
One coin.

SPACE
A space large enough for two lines of team members to face each other.

SAFETY
The ball must be placed between the two people at the end of each line so they will not injure each other going for the ball, and the person at the end of each line should kneel down on one knee. With aggressive athletes it may be better for them to sit on the ground facing each other.

GAME PLAN
Begin this activity by dividing the team into two equal teams. Have each team form a line and face the other team. The last person in each line should kneel on one knee or sit with the ball between them. Everyone except the first person in each line must close their eyes. This person is on the opposite end of the line from the ball. The members in each line join hands and a coin is tossed so the people at the front of the line can see it.

If the coin lands tails-up, nothing is done. If the coin lands heads-up, the sighted people squeeze the hand of the person next to them, and the squeeze goes down the line to the last person, who is on one knee or sitting. When this person feels the squeeze, she grabs the ball. The person who grabs the ball moves to the front of the line and becomes the sighted person and the coin is flipped again. This continues until one line moves up 5 people or a predetermined number of spots. A line must rotate backwards if members of that team get excited and squeeze when the coin indicates tails. If this happens, the sighted person also moves to the end of the line. It should also be noted that athletes must remain silent during this activity and avoid verbally warning teammates of a mistake or saying when to squeeze hands.

WRAP-UP
Was communication always clear?
If not, what problems did it cause?
How might this apply to our team and our need to communicate effectively?

LIGHTNING-FAST

GOAL
Highlight the importance of communication and goal-setting.

NUMBERS
9-15 is ideal. Consider dividing team into smaller subunits if more than 15.

EQUIPMENT
One tennis ball per team or subunit.

SPACE
Any area that is big enough for the team or subunits to form a circle.

SAFETY
No horseplay.
Have everyone be aware of each other's space.

GAME PLAN
Begin this activity by having the team or subunits form a circle. Give a tennis ball to one member of each team. Tell athletes that the person with the ball starts and stops the activity. Each member of the team is allowed to touch the ball only once. Only one person at a time is allowed to be in contact with the ball. Athletes are only allowed to use their hands to make contact with the ball. Athletes cannot give the ball to a teammate on either side of him. The group must remain in what they think is a circle throughout this activity. Once the group arrives at a solution for passing the ball, tell them that you will be timing the event. Have each team or subunit set a goal of a time to beat (a team of 12 can easily pass the ball in six seconds early in the activity). To see how your team will respond, tell them that their rival team has completed the activity in less than two seconds. After a few attempts and some brainstorming the group will arrive at a solution and perform the task very quickly.

WRAP-UP
There will most likely be a few athletes who will have negative reactions and will say things like, "There is no way we can do this in less than two seconds," or "That is impossible." This is a great time to ask your team their thoughts on the team goals that have been set for the current season.
Do some goals seem impossible?
What did it take to reach the goal in this activity?
How does that compare to the goals for our team?
How should we respond as a team when we are faced with what appears to be a daunting task?

VARIATIONS
Blindfold one or two members of each team or subunit to increase the need for communication and teamwork.

From Karl Rohnke, *The Bottomless Bag Again* (Kendall/Hunt Publishing, Dubuque, Iowa, 1994).

WORD STRING

GOAL
Highlight the importance of communication and encourage athletes to step outside their comfort zones.

NUMBERS
No limit, but at least 10 athletes is ideal.

EQUIPMENT
Enough blindfolds for each athlete to have one.

Athletes can simply close their eyes if you have no blindfolds (This can further emphasize the importance of trust among team members because they will be trusted to keep their eyes closed).

SPACE
An area that is half the size of a basketball court or larger.

SAFETY
Area must be free of obstacles.

Athletes must walk slowly and keep their hands up in front of them to avoid running into someone else.

GAME PLAN
This activity is similar to **Barnyard Music** on the following page, with a few different wrinkles. Begin the activity by having athletes get into pairs. Each pair should then come up with a "word string" (two or more words) that relates to your sport. For example, word strings for basketball could be "basketball hoop" and "jump shot." Once each pair arrives at a word string, they should share it with all of the other pairs. After all word strings have been heard, separate the pairs into opposite ends of the playing area and break the word string in half, giving one half to each team member (for example, "jump" and "shot"). Blindfold each of the athletes and then move some of the athletes around to cause more confusion. Once you give the signal to begin, pairs should attempt to locate each other. This is accomplished as a result of each half of the pair saying his part of the word string loud enough for the other half of the pair to hear. All athletes will be talking at the same time and it might be difficult for them to locate their partners. Once a pair is reunited, they may remove their blindfolds and move safely to the side.

WRAP-UP
Was it difficult to hear when everyone was talking at the same time?

What strategies did you use to find your partner?

What strategies can you use to block out irrelevant distractions when competing?

VARIATIONS
You can make the activity more challenging by placing three people on a team and have each threesome come up with a word string that contains three words. Then have them find each other as they did with two in a group.

Another way to increase the difficulty is to put athletes in larger groups. Then make up different phrases and have each group come back together and arrange themselves in the order of the words in the phrase you assigned them.

Contributed by Nicole Detling, Sport Psychology Doctoral Student, University of Utah.

BARNYARD MUSIC

GOAL

Highlight the importance of communication and encourage athletes to step outside their comfort zones.

NUMBERS

No limit, but at least 10 athletes is ideal.

EQUIPMENT

Enough blindfolds for each athlete to have one.

Athletes can simply close their eyes if you have no blindfolds (This can further emphasize the importance of trust among team members because they will be trusted to keep their eyes closed).

SPACE

An area that is half the size of a basketball court or larger.

SAFETY

Area must be free of obstacles.

Athletes must walk slowly and keep their hands up in front of them to avoid running into someone else.

GAME PLAN

Begin this activity by having athletes find a partner and form two lines by facing their partners. Once two lines are formed, each pair must come up with an animal sound that is distinct from any of the other sounds in the group. Allow athletes one or two minutes to arrive at a distinct animal sound and then let each pair demonstrate their sound to the rest of the team. Then have all athletes close their eyes or use blindfolds. Separate the pairs from each other by moving them to a different part of the activity area. Once each pair is separated, tell athletes to move slowly with their hands up in front of them and find their partner using only their animal sound. The pairs are allowed to have their sight back when they locate each other. Once they locate each other, the pair should move safely to the perimeter of the activity.

WRAP-UP

All of this can be paralleled back to the playing field. Communication is difficult when it's one-sided or not clear. Snakes hissing is much more difficult to find than cows mooing—like a quiet "pick left" called compared to "PICK LEFT!" There will be much laughter with this activity because most people don't walk around barking like a dog with their eyes closed. You might ask questions such as:

How many of you felt a bit silly while doing this activity?

What were the first few steps like when you walked with your eyes closed, compared to the last few before you found your partner?

How did it feel when you found your partner?

What would be the result if only one partner made the sound?

If we did this again would you pick a different sound?
How hard was it to keep your eyes shut?
Was there a sense of trust that everyone would keep their eyes closed?
What trust is needed in our sport?
Is this trust limited to the playing field?

VARIATION

Give team members pieces of paper with animal names (or pictures) on the paper. You will need at least two of each animal. Spread them out with their eyes closed and tell them to find the like animal, using only the animal's sound.

From Karl Rohnke, *Silver Bullets* (Project Adventure, Inc.: Beverly, MA, 1984).

BUILD THE COURT

GOAL
Reinforce the importance of communication among team members.

NUMBERS
10-15 is ideal. Consider dividing team into smaller subunits if more than 15.

EQUIPMENT
You will need approximately 50 pieces of material: items such as spoons, cups, golf tees, pencils, pieces of cardboard, clothespins, toy blocks, tinker toys, tongue-depressors, etc. The only stipulation is that there must be two identical sets of materials. You will also need a board or tray on which to build each project.

SPACE
Three areas are needed. These areas include a semi-private area for each half of the group, where they cannot see the other group, and a neutral area where the two groups can meet.

SAFETY
No horseplay.

GAME PLAN
This activity will require your athletes to use their imagination. To begin the activity, have the team divide in half and give each half the following written scenario:

As we begin this season, we discover that construction on the court or field is not finished. So, the team must build a place to practice and compete. The court/field must have bleachers and benches as well as goals and lines (if appropriate). But there is a problem. Each half of the team only has enough material to build half of the playing surface. In order to begin practicing on time, each half of the team must build half of the court or playing field and then bring both halves together. The halves should be mirror images of each other when they are brought together. To accomplish this task, the following sequence should be followed.

Begin this activity by giving the two halves of the team 5 minutes to begin building their halves of the court or field.

Bring the two groups together after the 5 minutes, but without their halves of the court or field. During this meeting, only one member from each group can talk. All members should come to the meeting, but no one else from either group should be allowed to talk or communicate with each other during this time. The two athletes that are allowed to talk should describe how their teams are building their half of the playing surface. The meeting should last no more than 90 seconds. After that time period, each team returns to its respective area for 5 minutes and continues its work. It will be important for each team to use the information it received in the previous meeting to make their its into a mirror image of the other team's.

This sequence should be continued until each athlete is a talking representative at least once. After everyone has had a chance to represent their group, the groups should bring their half of the court to the middle for comparison.

Following is an overview of the activity:
Each group must build identical court halves using the material provided.
Groups cannot view each other's half-court until the very end.
Groups come together periodically to discuss how they are building their half of the court.
Only one person from each group is allowed to communicate during each meeting.
No writing is allowed.

WRAP-UP

What were some of the problems that you encountered while building the court?

How often do we say something, assuming it is clear, only to find out the other person had no idea what we were saying?

How can we avoid this type of miscommunication on this team?

TEAM SUPPORT

GOAL
Demonstrate the importance of communication and trust.

NUMBERS
5-6 is ideal. Consider dividing the team into smaller subunits if more than 5 or 6.

EQUIPMENT
One roll of duct tape for each team.
One chair for each team.
A wall that can't be damaged with duct tape.
One long-sleeved shirt and a pair of long pants for each team (optional).

SPACE
Any space that has a wall that will not be damaged by duct tape.

SAFETY
The athlete on the wall must be spotted at all times so she will feel "protected."

GAME PLAN
Athletes will enjoy this activity because of its novelty and challenge. Begin by asking for a volunteer from each team to wear a long-sleeved shirt and long pants. Inform the team they will have a few minutes to devise a plan for taping their teammate to the wall in such a way that she will not fall. Once the planning period is finished, have the volunteer stand on a chair with her back against the wall. The remainder of the team will duct tape the volunteer to the wall using as much tape as needed to support the teammate when the chair is pulled out at the end of the time period.

WRAP-UP
How important was the planning time for this activity?
What did your team do to maximize the effectiveness of that time?
As the one taped to the wall, what did you feel like during the activity?
Did trust play a significant role in this activity?
How might this activity apply to our team?

VARIATIONS
Make the activity competitive if you have more than one team by seeing which team's volunteer can stay taped to the wall the longest.

From Karl Rohnke, *Funn Stuff II* (Kendall/Hunt, Dubuque, Iowa, 1996).

TEAM BLOB

GOAL
Demonstrate the importance of communication, leadership, trust, and co-operation while working towards a team goal.

NUMBERS
At least 8.

EQUIPMENT
One roll of masking tape.
Enough blindfolds for each athlete to have one.
Several pieces of equipment from your sport.

SPACE
A flat area that is about half of a basketball court.

SAFETY
Slow movement.
No horseplay.

GAME PLAN
This activity will allow one of your athletes to direct the team in its quest to achieve a goal. Begin by asking each member of the team to put on his blind-fold and then have everyone bunch together as closely as possible with hands down to the side. Once team members are as close as they can get, take the masking tape and wrap around the bunched-up team twice. Then place three or four pieces of the team's equipment in different locations within the activity area at least 20 feet from the group. After equipment is in place, allow the team to select a teammate to serve as the navigator. This person is then allowed to remove his blindfold. He must then direct the team to retrieve the objects without breaking the masking tape. If the tape is broken, the team must start over with the objects being placed in different places.

WRAP-UP
What problems did the team encounter?
Did individuals have to sacrifice anything to reach the team's goals?
How might this activity apply to situations on our team?

VARIATIONS
Have the entire team see where the objects are placed and then *all* put on their blindfolds to retrieve the object.
Have the pieces of equipment represent goals for the season.
Allow the team to choose more than one teammate to be the navigator.
Choose captains or others you want to observe in a leadership role.

Teamwork

KEEPER IN THE CAGE

GOAL
Reinforce the importance of teamwork and accountability among team members.

NUMBERS
No limit. Divide team into smaller subunits or teams of 6-10.

EQUIPMENT
None.

SPACE
Any area free of obstacles.

SAFETY
N/A.

GAME PLAN
This activity will take some explanation on your part, but athletes will have a lot of fun once they figure it out. Begin by dividing teams into groups of 6-10. Have each team form a circle where team members are facing each other. One athlete will then be designated to be the "keeper in the cage" and move to the middle of the circle. Once you have this arrangement, you will need to describe in detail how the game works.

The keeper in the cage will randomly point to any athlete in the circle and say one of three animals: Giraffe, Hippo or Elephant. Depending on which animal is chosen, athletes will do one of the following sequences.

Giraffe—Stand with hands together stretched overhead to represent the neck. Athletes immediately to this athlete's right or left will fall to hands and knees and crouch near this athlete to serve as the legs for the giraffe.

Hippo—Turn 180 degrees and bend over with rear end facing in towards the middle of the circle. Athletes immediately to this athlete's right and left will put middle finger on top of index finger, try to bend index finger and then place them by this athlete's head to serve as ears. (Note: You might avoid having the athlete turn around and bend over if you have a young team. You can simply have him or her bend over with head facing the middle of the circle.)

Elephant—Put both arms together out in front of his face to represent the trunk. Athletes immediately to his right and left must form a large "C" with their arms and put them next to his head to serve as ears.

Athletes should begin the game once you feel you have adequately explained the actions of each animal and they have had a chance to practice a few times. The keeper randomly points to a person, and this person along with those immediately next to him must perform the appropriate action before the keeper can count to ten. The keeper should count very quickly. If any one of the three athletes involved in the actions makes a mistake or doesn't get into position in time, the person who was pointed to must come to the middle to be the keeper. This person must be the keeper regardless of whether he made the mistake. Continue the game long enough for everyone to serve as the keeper.

WRAP-UP

Was it important to be able to concentrate and react quickly in this game?

When is that important to be successful in our sport?

Was there any communication involved in this game?

What was significant about having to be keeper even when you weren't necessarily the one who made the mistake?

How does that apply to our team?

What ways can members of a team "let each other down"?

From Aynsley Smith, *Powerplay: Mental Toughness for Hockey and Beyond* (Athletic Guide Publishing: Flagler Beach, Florida, 1999).

WACKY BASEBALL

GOAL
Reinforce the importance of teamwork and communication among team members.

NUMBERS
12-30.

EQUIPMENT
Soft sponge ball and bat (the ball does not need to travel more than 30-40 feet when hit).

SPACE
Flat area about half the size of a basketball court.

SAFETY
No horseplay.

GAME PLAN
Begin this activity by dividing team into equal smaller teams, with one designated as the hitting team and the other one as the fielding team. Inform the teams they are playing Wacky Baseball and there are a few rules to follow when playing. The team at bat can score runs by the batter hitting the ball and running around the remainder of the team. Each time he runs a lap around the team, it is one run. The team will soon learn that the closer they stand, the more runs their team will score. In order to get the batter out, the fielding team must get in a single file line with everyone facing the same direction. The first athlete in line must pass the ball backwards between his legs to the next athlete in line. This continues until the last athlete in line receives the ball. He must then run with the ball and hand it to the first person in line. The batter is officially out when the first athlete in line receives the ball again. All athletes should hit before switching sides if you have a small team. Consider allowing half of the team to hit if your team is large. Play as many innings as time allows.

WRAP-UP
What strategies did your team use to increase your efficiency?
Was communication important to be successful? If so, how?
What were your reactions when you were told the winning team was the one with the fewest runs? (See variation below.)
Can our sport be "unfair" at times? If so, how should we respond?

VARIATIONS
Once the game is finished, ask how many runs each team scored. Observe what reactions you get from your athletes by announcing that in Wacky Baseball, the winning team is the one that scores the fewest runs. This will lead into the discussion on how the team should handle situations that are perceived to be unfair.

From Karl Rohnke, *Funn Stuff III* (Kendall/Hunt Publishing: Dubuque, Iowa, 1998).

BALLOON CHALLENGE

GOAL
Reinforce the importance of teamwork and communication among team members.

NUMBERS
No limit. Divide the team into subunits of 4-6 athletes.

EQUIPMENT
One balloon for each athlete.
Markers for beginning and finish points of a course.

SPACE
Any open space free of obstacles.

SAFETY
No horseplay.

GAME PLAN
This activity will require your athletes to be creative in how they work together to accomplish a relatively easy task. Begin by dividing athletes into teams or subunits of 4-6 athletes. Each athlete should inflate her balloon. Once balloons are inflated, inform teams that their goal is to move together as one unit from the starting point to the finish marker as quickly as possible while keeping all balloons from touching the ground. As the team progresses from the start to the finish, no one is allowed to touch a balloon with any part of her body except the torso. Therefore, they cannot allow the balloons to touch any part of their hands, arms or legs. The team must start over if anyone touches a balloon with any part of her body other than the torso, or if a balloon touches the ground.

WRAP-UP
What strategies did your team use to be successful?
How important was it that your team worked well together?
Were any of you tempted to cheat during this activity?
How can cheating affect our team in a negative way?

VARIATIONS
Require two athletes on each team to be in contact with all balloons on their team at all times.
Require three athletes on each team to be in contact with all balloons on their team at all times.

REVERSE-ORDER STEPPING-STONES

GOAL
Encourage teamwork and communication among team members.

NUMBERS
10-15 is ideal. Divide team into smaller subunits if more than 15.

EQUIPMENT
One piece of 8.5" x 11" paper and small piece of duct tape for each athlete.

SPACE
Area about a quarter of the size of a basketball court.

SAFETY
No horseplay.
Athletes should not be allowed to lift each other in any manner.

GAME PLAN
This can be a very effective teambuilding activity if athletes on the team are having conflicts with each other because they will be required to invade each other's "personal space" to accomplish a goal. Begin by giving each athlete a piece of paper and a piece of duct tape. Have athletes on the team or each subunit form a line where they are facing the same way and are shoulder to shoulder. Each athlete should then tape his piece of paper on the floor in front of him and step on it. The objective of the activity is for the team to completely reverse the order they start in so that the line is a mirror image of itself when they are finished. For example, the athlete on the far left should be the athlete on the far right when finished. The second athlete on the right at the start should be the second athlete from the left when finished. Athletes are only allowed to step on the paper, and are not allowed to touch the floor with any part of their bodies as they attempt this activity. If any athlete touches the floor, the entire team must begin again.

WRAP-UP
What was your initial response when you were told what the team had to accomplish?
What were the keys to success in this activity?
How important was communication?
What was the response if someone touched the floor and the team had to start again at the beginning?

VARIATIONS
Provide the team with one extra piece of paper (11 for a team of 10 athletes) to use while attempting to accomplish their goal.
Provide a creative scenario such as that the team must cross a narrow bridge across a deep ravine without anyone falling and getting injured.

From Karl Rohnke, *Silver Bullets* (Project Adventure, Inc.: Beverly, MA, 1984).

STRETCHING IT

GOAL
Reinforce the importance of communication and using imagination to stretch beyond previous limits.

NUMBERS
10-30 is ideal.

EQUIPMENT
Props such as ropes, string or cloth.
A marker such as a flag.

SPACE
Depending on the size of the team and the number of props, the space needed could be up to a football field in length.

SAFETY
No horseplay.

GAME PLAN
The old adage that a chain is only as strong as its weakest link will be vividly presented in this activity. Begin the activity by telling your team the objective of this activity is for them to depend on each other to see how far the team can stretch itself while staying connected to each other using the props provided. Give the team 5 minutes to devise a plan to determine how they can utilize their own bodies and the props that are provided to stretch from a designated starting point out to a point where the last person places the flag as a marker. After the marker is placed on the ground, the team comes back to the starting point. Give them another short time period to plan their next attempt. The team then attempts to stretch again to beat their previous mark. This can be repeated as many times as necessary until they feel they have reached their limit. Remind them that the team must start over each time they lose a connection anywhere along the line of athletes and props.

WRAP-UP
How did the team stretch as far as it did?

What did the team do differently from the first attempt to the last time you placed your mark on ground?

How can the changes made here parallel the changes that will be made during a season for us?

Staying connected was a key to success in this activity. How does our team need to stay connected to reach our goals?

What does the phrase, "a chain is only as strong as its weakest link" mean to you? How does it apply to this activity and to our team?

From Jim Cain and Barry Jolliff, *Teamwork and Teamplay* (Kendall/Hunt Publishing: Dubuque, Iowa, 1998).

ALLIGATOR POND

GOAL
Encourage teamwork, communication and problem solving among team members.

NUMBERS
No limit. Divide team into smaller subunits if the team is large.

EQUIPMENT
Enough pieces of paper (8.5" x 11") or carpet squares of similar size for each athlete to have one.

SPACE
Area marked with boundaries that represent an alligator pond.

SAFETY
N/A.

GAME PLAN
Inform athletes the objective of this game is for the team or subunit to work together to get everyone across the alligator pond without falling into the water. Begin by giving each athlete one piece of paper or carpet square to represent a lily pad, and then have everyone go to one side of the pond. Remind them that each athlete must *always* remain in contact with her lily pad as the team begins to move across the pond. Often athletes will place a lily pad down with a hand and then step on it without maintaining contact. If an athlete does this or loses contact with it at any time, the team loses that lily pad. The team must also start over from the beginning. In addition, the team must start over from the beginning if anyone allows any part her body to touch the alligator pond at any time.

WRAP-UP
What were the keys for being successful in this activity?
What was the response if someone forgot to maintain constant contact with her lily pad or touched the alligator pond?
What is the proper response to make if a teammate makes a mistake in a game?
Do all athletes respond to the same types of feedback from their teammates?

Contributed by Nicole Detling, Sport Psychology doctoral student, University of Utah.

ACTIVITY BUDDY

GOAL
Help reduce cliques on your team and encourage athletes to step outside their social comfort zones.

NUMBERS
No limit.

EQUIPMENT
Slips of paper with athlete names and activities.

SPACE
Locker room, classroom or any space where athletes will not be disturbed.

SAFETY
N/A.

GAME PLAN
Before beginning this activity, decide on several activities around a particular theme your athletes can do with a partner. For example, one theme could be "giving back to the team" or another theme could be "getting to know more about the town or city surrounding your school." You will need one activity for each pair of athletes on your team. Examples of activities where athletes give back to the team might include compiling a CD inspired by the personalities on the team, constructing valentines for everyone on the team (staff included), e-mailing signed recruits with congratulations and news of what is going on with the team, baking holiday cookies for the team, designing a birthday card extending birthday wishes from the team (it would be a card the team signs for birthdays), creating a "commercial" for the team like the "priceless" campaign for Visa credit card. You want activities that will encourage sufficient interaction, problem-solving and teamwork, not just superficial activities. Write these activities down on slips of paper and put them in a hat.

Once you have established the theme and appropriate activities, divide athletes into two equal groups. Because athletes will be divided again, they should be in the same group with other athletes they tend to socialize with on a regular basis. For example, you can group athletes by class (seniors and juniors in one group, freshmen and sophomores in the other group), proximity of lockers in the locker room or any other fashion where athletes are with others they "hang out" with regularly. Once you have two equal groups, write the names of each athlete from one group on separate slips of paper (one for each athlete). Put those names in a hat. Members of the other group should then draw names from the hat to establish pairs. After pairs are established, have the athlete who did not choose from the name hat select an activity from the activity hat.

Pairs will have one month to accomplish their tasks and report back to the team on how it went. Results of the activities may well be observed before the end of the month.

WRAP-UP
What was the most rewarding aspect of this experience?
How important is it that we know each of the members of the team?
How will this activity transfer to our team when we are competing?

VARIATIONS
Have a different theme for each month or time period you choose.

Contributed by Shelley Johnson, Assistant Coach, University of North Carolina Field Hockey.

PROBLEM-SOLVING

GOAL
To encourage team members to work together to accomplish a goal, "think outside the box," and realize that obvious solutions aren't always correct.

NUMBERS
12-16 is ideal.

EQUIPMENT
Enough pieces of paper for each athlete to have one.

SPACE
Any open space that is free of obstacles.

SAFETY
N/A.

GAME PLAN
Divide the team into groups of four. Each team gets four pieces of paper, and each paper has one of the following numbers on it: 1, 2, 5 or 10. Each athlete should pick a number. The goal of this activity is for each team to get everyone from side A of a "canyon" to side B. The following rules must be followed when attempting to accomplish this goal.

Athletes must cross in pairs.

Once each pair crosses to side B, one athlete goes back to side A and then another pair crosses to side B.

Athletes should continue crossing following this pattern until all 4 team members end up on side B. Remember, they must always cross in pairs and go back as singles.

Each team must have their total score equal 17. To accomplish this, the following scoring formula is used.

Each time a pair crosses the canyon to side B, the highest number counts (Example: If 10 and 2 cross, 10 points is counted towards the total).

Of those two athletes, the lowest number (e.g., 2) goes back to side A. That athlete's number will again be counted towards the total.

Then the next two athletes cross to side B and the highest of those two numbers counts.

The lowest number on side B must return to side A etc.

Key:

1 & 2 cross = 2 points	2 points total
1 returns = 1 point	3 points total
5 & 10 cross = 10 points	13 points total
2 returns = 2 points	15 points total
1 & 2 cross = 2 points	17 points total

WRAP-UP

What were some of the frustrations you felt during this activity?

What were a few keys to successfully accomplishing this goal?

How might this activity be applied to our team and what we want to accomplish?

Contributed by Nicole Detling, Sport Psychology doctoral student, University of Utah.

SHOESTRING CHALLENGE

GOAL
Encourage teamwork and communication among team members during a challenging activity.

NUMBERS
At least 8 is ideal, but divide larger team into smaller subunits.

EQUIPMENT
None.

SPACE
An area about a quarter the size of a basketball court.

SAFETY
Remind athletes to avoid kicking each other.

GAME PLAN
This activity will challenge your athletes to be creative and communicate well with each other. Begin by dividing the team into smaller teams or subunits of at least four athletes. Tell anyone that has double knots in their shoestrings to tie them into regular knots. Instruct athletes to lie on the floor as teams with their legs in the air. When you say "go," each team tries to untie all of the shoes on their team before any of the other teams can do it. At no time are athletes allowed to use their hands. Their feet must stay off the ground throughout the activity.

WRAP-UP
Was this activity frustrating? Why or why not?
Could any of you have done this activity on your own?
How were you able to help each other?
How do we rely on each other on our team?
How can we make sure we are always willing and able to help our team-
mates?

From Alana Jones, *Team Building Activities for Every Group* (Rec Room Publishing: Richland, Washington, 1999).

Yurt Circle

Goal
Reinforce the importance of trust and the idea that a chain is only as strong as its weakest link.

Numbers
8-10 is ideal. Divide team into smaller subunits if more than 10.

Equipment
None.

Space
Area about a quarter the size of a basketball court.

Safety
No horseplay.

Game Plan
Begin this activity by having team members form groups of 8-10. Ask them to form a circle with their teammates, hold hands and then count off by twos. Once everyone has a number, tell athletes with the number 1 to lean in and athletes with the number 2 to lean out. Athletes should keep their feet on the ground and lean forward or backwards without bending at the waist. All athletes should continue to hold hands as this occurs. After the team has been holding this pose for several moments, tell them to switch positions. This action should be one fluid motion with everyone moving at the same time. If anyone lets go at any time, it will be difficult for teammates to compensate and the circle will be broken. Athletes will have to compensate for the difference in size of teammates within a circle as well.

Wrap-Up
What role did communication (particularly listening) play in this activity?
What happened if someone let go?
How does this relate to our team and the importance of everyone doing their part?
How did the team members "compensate" for each other during this activity?

From Aynsley Smith, *Powerplay: Mental Toughness for Hockey and Beyond* (Athletic Guide Publishing: Flagler Beach, Florida, 1999).

TEAM WEB

GOAL
Emphasize the importance of planning, trust and communication among teammates.

NUMBERS
8-15 is ideal.

EQUIPMENT
A large ball of string.
A soft surface such as a tumbling mat or mulch if outside.
Two volleyball standards or other devices on which to tie the web such as goal posts or trees.

SPACE
An area large enough to build the web described below.

SAFETY
Team members must always keep their hands on the athlete being passed through the web. The athlete's feet should never be higher than her head and her back should always be toward the ground as she is being passed through the web. Team members cannot jump or be thrown through the web.

GAME PLAN
Before beginning this activity, you must build a web between two standards using the ball of string. The bottom of the web should be about waist high for the athletes and as tall as the tallest athlete on your team. The spaces in the web should be large enough for athletes to be able to pass through without touching the sides. Vary the size and shape of the spaces to increase the difficulty of the challenge. The object of this activity is for team members to work together to help each athlete through the web without touching any part of the web. When a team member is going through the web she must always be in contact with the ground or other team members. The goal is accomplished when all teammates move through the web from one side to the other.

WRAP-UP
How did the team reach the goal?
What part did each team member play?
What part did the person going through the web play?
Can you think of times when our team will need to depend on each other like this?

VARIATIONS
Divide the team in half and require the two halves to start on either side of the web. Both groups must work together to get each athlete to the opposite side from where she started. You might allow a designated number of touches to the web (e.g., three) if the team struggles too much with no touches.

Depending on the number of participants and spaces in the web, it might be more challenging to limit the number of passes a team can make through one space. Otherwise a team might pass everyone through a lower or larger space.

From Karl Rohnke, *Silver Bullets* (Project Adventure, Inc.: Beverly, MA, 1984).

INNER TUBE CHALLENGE

GOAL
Encourage teamwork and communication among team members when faced with a difficult task.

NUMBERS
8-15 is ideal. Divide team into smaller subunits if larger than 15.

EQUIPMENT
Four used bicycle inner tubes.
Two large (#10 or 1-lb) coffee cans.

SPACE
Area about half the size of a basketball court.
You might think about conducting the activity outside if you are concerned about getting the floor wet.

SAFETY
No horseplay.

GAME PLAN
Team members will be challenged to be creative and "think outside the box" to accomplish this task. Begin by drawing a circle on the ground about 15 feet in diameter. Place a coffee can that is half-full of water in the middle of the circle. Give the team four old bicycle inner tubes and tell them they are to use the tubes to retrieve the can and move it to a location outside the circle. Inform them they must be creative in how they connect the inner tubes to move the can of water. While attempting to do this, no athlete is allowed to have any part of his body cross the line into the inside of the circle at any time. In addition, athletes are not allowed to touch the can with any body part during this activity. The team must put the can back in the middle if any of the water is spilled or anyone crosses the line into the inside of the circle. The team can use the second can to practice on before they attempt to retrieve the can in the middle of the circle.

WRAP-UP
How did the team plan for this activity?
What was the most difficult part of this activity?
How does our team have to plan for success?
How important was communication in this activity?
When are the most crucial times for communication on our team?

VARIATION
Require the team to retrieve the can from the middle and empty it into the second can outside the circle without spilling any of the water.

From Alana Jones, *Team Building Activities for Every Group* (Rec Room Publishing: Richland, WA, 1999).

Balloon Train

Goal
Reinforce the importance of teamwork and communication.

Numbers
12-16 is ideal. Consider breaking team into smaller subunits if more than 16.

Equipment
One basketball-sized balloon for each athlete, plus a few extras in case some burst.

Space
Any open space.

Safety
No horseplay.

Game Plan
This is a great teambuilding activity that involves many of the elements of a team working together. Begin by having each athlete blow up a balloon. To conduct this activity, the team will need one less balloon than there are athletes (if the team consists of ten athletes, you will need nine balloons). Have the athletes place their balloons on the ground, and designate an area about 50 feet away from the starting point as the "deposit point." This area can be a square on the floor that represents a soccer goal or a large trashcan that represents a basket, etc. Team members should then get into a single file line with everyone facing the "deposit point." The objective is for the team to move the balloons from the starting area to the finish and deposit them in their chosen goal without letting the balloons touch the floor. However, athletes may not touch the balloons with their hands, arms or heads and they must transport the balloons together in a line with the balloons held between athletes at their waistline. Athletes should place their hands on the shoulders of the person in front of them to help maintain contact and to avoid touching a balloon with anything other than their torsos. The team cannot leave the starting point until all team members are together. If the balloons touch the floor, hands, arms or head the entire team starts over.

Wrap-Up
Was there anything difficult about this activity?
How did you have to handle the balloons?
Are there any parallels to handling the balloons and taking care of the ball in your sport? If there is failure how does it feel to fail?
What do you have to do after you fail as an individual athlete?
What does the team have to do after a team failure?

From Karl Rohnke and Steve Butler, *Quicksilver* (Kendall/Hunt Publishing: Dubuque, Iowa, 1995)

TEAM JUGGLE

GOAL
Emphasize the importance of concentration and teamwork.

NUMBER
6-8 is ideal. Consider dividing team into smaller subunits if more than 8.

EQUIPMENT
Two to four soft objects athletes can toss to one another.
Two to four tennis balls, or balls used by the team in its sport.

SPACE
An area large enough for the team or subunits to form circles and safely throw the objects.

SAFETY
All objects are tossed softly, underhanded, in a safe manner.

GAME PLAN
Athletes must be able to communicate with each other while concentrating on the task at hand to successfully complete this activity. Begin by having athletes form circles of equal numbers. One athlete in each circle is designated the starter. He starts the activity by tossing a soft object to a member of the team. That team member then tosses the object to another team member and this continues until the entire team has had the object once. At this time it is tossed back to the starter. Tell the team that they will be developing a pattern and that they need to remember the athlete they tossed the object to and who they got it from. The rules are that an athlete cannot toss the ball to an athlete on either side of him when establishing the pattern and the team should make every attempt to always catch the objects. The same pattern will be used throughout the activity. Using one soft object, go through the pattern 2 or 3 times so the team knows the pattern. Once everyone has learned the pattern and is able to consistently catch the object, add another ball into the pattern by having the starter toss it immediately after the first object is tossed. The group will now have two objects in the pattern. After they are able to successfully go through the entire pattern a few times, add a third similar object as was done with the second object. Allow them to see how many times they can progress through the entire pattern without making a mistake.

WRAP-UP
Were there any mistakes?
What were some of the responses when someone made a mistake?
What caused those mistakes?
How were they corrected?
Did your team improve the more you went through the pattern? Why?
How important is concentration in our sport?

VARIATIONS
Introduce objects of different sizes into the pattern.
Reverse the pattern.
Toss one set of objects forward through the pattern and the other set of objects in a reverse pattern at the same time.
Have the team members rotate to another spot in the circle and do it again until they are successful. Depending on the skill of the group, 4 or 5 objects may be needed.
Make eye contact with the person you are throwing to each time.
After the team gets several balls going, stop the team and ask them to discuss the keys to success for their team. Write those "keys" on the balls and have the team juggle again. Once one of the balls is dropped, stop the team and ask athletes what happens when they "drop the ball" in that important area of success.

Portions of this activity were contributed by Dan Gould, Professor and Sport Psychology Consultant at Michigan State University.

FLIP FLOP

GOAL
Reinforce the importance of teamwork and communication.

NUMBERS
Less than 15 is ideal. Consider dividing team into smaller subunits if more than 15.

EQUIPMENT
Tarp or blanket with dimensions of about 4 x 8 feet.

SPACE
Small area the size of a classroom or a quarter of a basketball court.

SAFETY
Team members should not be allowed to get on each other's shoulders or jump in any manner.

GAME PLAN
This is a simple activity that can be very challenging if team members aren't willing to discuss the possibilities before beginning. Begin this activity by having all team members stand on the tarp. Once everyone is on the tarp, they must turn the tarp over and stand on the other side. The key point to make during this activity is that they can only touch the tarp. The team must start again if any team member touches the floor.

WRAP-UP
What did the team have to do to accomplish the goal?
What were the responses if someone touched the floor?
How can this activity apply to what we have to do as a team to be successful?

VARIATIONS
Have subunits compete with each other to see who can accomplish the task the quickest.

From Karl Rohnke, *Funn Stuff III* (Kendall/Hunt Publishing: Dubuque, Iowa, 1998).

BLIND SPELL

GOAL
Help your team realize the importance of teamwork and to funnel their competitive spirit in the right direction.

NUMBERS
15-45 is ideal. This activity works well with large teams.

EQUIPMENT
Enough rope or other material to mark off boundaries and benches.
One Magic Marker.
Enough tennis balls to spell words such as "teamwork," "trust," "communication" or anything else that may be needed for your team, one tennis ball per letter.
Extra tennis balls scattered on the playing field add to the challenge.
Blindfolds for half of the team members.

SPACE
Large area about half the size of a basketball court.
Can be conducted inside or outside.

SAFETY
No running should be allowed during this activity and hands (bumpers) must be up in front of people when they walk blindfolded. Have two or three athletes on the playing field to prevent players from bumping into each other.

GAME PLAN
Before beginning this activity, you should spell the word "teamwork" (or another aspect of your team you feel is important) four times. Use one ball for each letter. Consequently, you will need 32 tennis balls to spell "teamwork" four different times. Mark an area about the size of half of a basketball court with four small "bench" areas on the outside of the large area. The benches should be approximately 6 to 8 feet long so 4 or 5 team members can stand inside them. Divide your team into four smaller teams and assign a bench for each team. Once each team is assigned a bench, they must divide themselves by having half of the athletes serve as play-ers on the field and half of the athletes on the bench. The players on the field must then be blindfolded. Once all players on the field are blindfolded, scatter the tennis balls with the letters on them on the area inside the boundaries. Explain this activ-ity by telling the teams that for them to accomplish an outcome goal such as win-ning the conference championship, every team must spell the word "teamwork." The four players on the bench must stay on the bench and verbally guide the blind-folded players to get the tennis balls. The blindfolded players must lay the balls in front of the bench spelling the word. The sighted players on the bench cannot touch the tennis balls but can only guide the blindfolded players. Even though the goal is not accomplished until all teams spell their word properly, this activity usually becomes very competitive with each team trying to spell their word and not helping the other teams.

WRAP-UP
How did we reach our goal?
What could we have done differently to accomplish this goal?
Was it difficult to hear directions from your team?
How can this activity be applied to what we have to do as a team to be successful?

TIN CAN TRANSFER

GOAL
Emphasize the importance of teamwork and communication.

NUMBERS
10-25 is ideal. Consider dividing team into subunits if more than 25.

EQUIPMENT
Two or three large (#10 or 1-lb) coffee cans.

SPACE
An area the size of a quarter of a basketball court.

SAFETY
No kicking the cans.

GAME PLAN
Teammates will be forced to rely heavily on each other to accomplish this task. Begin by having the team or subunits form a circle. Place one can on the ground/floor in front of one of the team members. This athlete is designated the starter. The objective is for the team or each subunit to pass the tin can from the starter around the circle and back again. The can must be passed in order from athlete to athlete so that everyone possesses and controls the can. It may not touch the ground and athletes must only touch the can with their feet and legs. They are also forbidden from allowing anything other than their feet to touch the ground. If the can touches the ground or is touched with a body part other than the feet or legs, the team must start over from the beginning. After successfully passing one tin can, you can have the team pass two cans simultaneously in opposite directions. This will cause one athlete to possess both cans at the same time.

WRAP-UP
What did each team member have to do to reach the goal?
Did the team drop the can? If so, why?
Was it just one person's fault?
What did you learn from this activity?
How can it be applied to what our team must do to be successful?

VARIATIONS
Use other objects such as soccer balls, basketballs or volleyballs.
Mix the objects that teams or subunits must use at one time.
Create a competition by timing the team or having subunits compete with each other.

From Karl Rohnke, *Bottomless Bag Again* (Kendall/Hunt Publishing: Dubuque, Iowa, 1994).

Dependent Pairs Tag

GOAL
Encourage teamwork and communication between two teammates.

NUMBERS
10-30 is ideal. Consider dividing team into smaller subunits if more than 30.

EQUIPMENT
Several small sponge balls or rolled-up socks.
Enough blindfolds for half of the athletes.

SPACE
Area that is at least half the size of a basketball court.
Area can be smaller if you have fewer than 20 athletes.

SAFETY
No pushing, running or diving allowed.
A sighted person must always assist the blindfolded partner when he is bending over to pick up the ball or sock so that he does not bump heads with another athlete.

GAME PLAN
This is an excellent activity for requiring two athletes on a team to work together. It has the potential to be very effective with teammates who haven't been working well together. Begin by having each team member get a partner. One of the partners should wear a blindfold. Once one person is blindfolded, give each pair a "nugget" (soft object). The sighted person must verbally guide the blindfolded person to throw the object in order to hit another athlete with it. If the athlete throwing the nugget misses, he must be verbally guided to the object to retrieve it and throw again. The object of the game is to avoid being hit while hitting the other athletes who have been blindfolded. Once a blindfolded athlete has been hit 10 times, that pair must move to the sidelines and watch.

WRAP-UP
How clear were the directions you were given?
Did the directions improve as the game progressed?
Did you become frustrated? Was anyone at fault?
How can we make sure our communication improves throughout the season?

From Karl Rohnke, *Bottomless Bag Again* (Kendall/Hunt Publishing: Dubuque, Iowa, 1994).

TEAM PYRAMID

GOAL
Reinforce the importance of teamwork, communication and dealing effectively with adversity.

NUMBERS
8-15 is ideal. Consider dividing team into smaller subunits if more than 15.

EQUIPMENT
35 tennis balls per team or subunit.
Rough surface such as carpet squares or carpeted area so tennis balls won't slide when stacked.

SPACE
Carpeted area or area where another rough surface can be used.

SAFETY
No horseplay.

GAME PLAN
This is a simple but challenging activity that will require a specific strategy from team members. Begin by giving each member of the team an equal number of tennis balls. Have team members stand around the designated area (carpet square). Tell them the objective for the team is to build a three-sided pyramid in a designated time. The structure must be built five tennis balls high. The team must start over if the structure falls. Finally, mark one ball to be placed on top. The top ball can represent the league championship or some other ultimate team goal.

WRAP-UP
Did your team encounter any problems?
Did anyone make a mistake?
If so, how did the rest of the team feel when that occurred?
What changes did the team make after a failure?
Did you learn and move on, or did you dwell on it?
What do you do during competition?
Are there any other ways this structure and method of construction relate to our team?

VARIATIONS
To increase the difficulty of the task, you can designate a "blind area" around the carpet. When a team member is in that area, he is blindfolded and must rely on team members to help. It is probably best not to time the team or have competition between subunits when using the "blind area" as part of the requirements.

SPOKES IN THE WHEEL

GOAL
Encourage teamwork and emphasize the importance of every role on the team when attempting to reach a goal.

NUMBERS
8-12 is ideal. Consider dividing team into smaller subunits if more than 12.

EQUIPMENT
Heavy duty rubber band or bicycle inner tube.
Rope or string cut into segments of 12-15 feet.
Large plastic cup.
Large ball (can be from your sport).

SPACE
Area the size of a regulation basketball court.

SAFETY
No horseplay or jerking the ropes.

GAME PLAN
This is an excellent activity for demonstrating how every team member is important for the overall success of a team. Begin by tying the rope or string segments to the rubber band or inner tube so that it looks like a giant wheel hub with spokes. Place the ball on the rubber band in the middle with athletes holding the end of each rope at least 10 feet away from the ball. The goal is for the team or each subunit to pick the ball up off the ground, carry it to the cup (distance is determined by available space and how difficult you want to make it) and place it on the cup without dropping the ball or knocking over the cup. If the ball is dropped or the cup knocked over, a foul is called, and the team must start over.

WRAP-UP
How would you describe the planning period your team or subunit used for this activity?
What happened if one of the team members pulled on his or her rope too much?
Was there a problem when someone let go or did not carry his or her weight?
How does this relate to our team and our goals?

VARIATIONS
Have athletes get into pairs. Blindfold one of them and have that athlete hold the string or rope. The other athlete in that pair must communicate with her to move in the proper direction. You might also put chairs in the team's path and refer to the chairs as an opponent or an obstacle that might occur during the season.

From Jim Cain and Barry Jolliff, *Teamwork and Teamplay* (Kendall/Hunt Publishing: Dubuque, Iowa, 1998).

BUNGEE CHALLENGE

GOAL
Reinforce the importance of teamwork and communication.

NUMBERS
8-15 is ideal. Consider dividing the team into smaller subunits if more than 15.

EQUIPMENT
One bungee cord that is 14 to 20 inches in length and tied to make a circle. It must be strong and free of sharp edges.

SPACE
Any open space.

SAFETY
No horseplay.

GAME PLAN
Athletes will enjoy the challenge of this teambuilding activity. Begin by having the team or each subunit join hands in a line or a circle. Inform them that the goal of the activity is for the team to work together so that everyone passes through the bungee cord one at a time without anyone breaking their hold with the teammate next to them. If the team forms a line you should lay the cord on the ground. If they form a circle, you should put the cord over one person's arm and tell the team they must all pass through it. To make the task more difficult, you can make the rule that the person going through the hole may not touch the cord with any part of her body. The team will have to pull the cord in a manner that allows each of their teammates to reach an individual objective as well as working toward a team objective.

WRAP-UP
For each team member to be successful what did that person have to do? What did the team have to do?

Was everyone always directly involved?

How can this relate to what we have to do to accomplish our individual and team goals?

VARIATIONS
Blindfold one or two team members from the team or subunit to increase the need for communication and teamwork.

From Jim Cain and Barry Jolliff, *Teamwork and Teamplay* (Kendall/Hunt Publishing, 1998).

BALANCE

GOAL
Reinforce the importance of teamwork and communication.

NUMBERS
8-12 is ideal. Consider dividing team into smaller subunits if more than 12.

EQUIPMENT
Lightweight dowel or pole 6' to 8' long and two large washers that fit loosely around the pole.

SPACE
Any space is suitable for this activity.

SAFETY
Remind athletes to avoid horseplay with the pole.

GAME PLAN
Team members will need to have precise communication and a high level of teamwork to successfully accomplish this task. Begin by placing one washer on each end of the pole. Then instruct each team member to place one or two straight fingers parallel to the ground (palm of the hand facing up) under the pole and hold the pole steady at about 5 feet off the ground. Athletes are then instructed to work together to lower the pole to the ground without dropping a washer off either end. The challenge here will be for all team members to communicate with each other to lower themselves at the same rate to avoid having a washer fall to the ground. The team must start over if anyone loses contact with the pole or a washer falls off the end.

WRAP UP
Was it important for each team member to do his part?
What happens when one teammate isn't willing to do his part or "carry his part of the load" for this team?
You had to work together to balance the pole in this activity. How is balance significant in our quest for excellence?

VARIATION
Blindfold some of the members of each subunit.
Create a competition if you have more than one team or subunit.

From Karl Rohnke, *Funn Stuff IV* (Kendall/Hunt Publishing: Dubuque, Iowa, 2000).

NAVIGATING OBSTACLES

GOAL
Reinforce the importance of teamwork and properly handling obstacles.

NUMBERS
10-15 is ideal. Consider dividing team into smaller subunits if more than 15.

EQUIPMENT
Line on the floor or field (several strips of masking tape side by side or the sideline marking of a football field would be ideal).

SPACE
Any open space. You will need to put a line on the floor that is approximately 30 feet long.

SAFETY
The area must be free of obstacles, and team members cannot stack or lift each other.

GAME PLAN
Begin this challenging but fun activity by having team members divide into two equal teams. Each team should stand on one end of the line(about 30 feet long), facing the other team. The goal for this activity is for both teams to move simultaneously from the end of the line where they started to the other end of the line. Teams will have to bypass each other on the way to the opposite end of the line. Once the teams begin to move toward each other, athletes must always have at least one foot in contact with the line. If an athlete's foot touches the ground on either side of the line, the foot must also be in touch with the line. If not, the entire team must start over from beginning. Feet are the only parts of the body that are allowed to be in contact with the line or the ground. Athletes will have to rely on each other to successfully accomplish this task.

WRAP-UP
What were some of the difficulties your team faced?
What did it take to accomplish your goal?
What part did each of you play in reaching this goal?
How might this activity relate to what we might face in our quest for a successful season?

VARIATIONS
Blindfold half of the members of each team to increase the reliance on each other for success.

TEAM TAG

GOAL
Reinforce the importance of teamwork.

NUMBERS
12 or more.

EQUIPMENT
A soft ball (e.g., Nerf ball).

SPACE
An area about half the size of a basketball court can be used. This area should have boundaries on each side. Basketball court lines can be used to designate the area.

SAFETY
The area used should be safe to run on and free of any obstacles. The ball that is used must be soft. Athletes can only tag below the shoulders (i.e., no face).

GAME PLAN
The need for teamwork in this activity will increase as it progresses. Athletes should be made to follow a few simple rules when participating. To begin the activity, one athlete throws the ball and attempts to "tag" another athlete by hitting her with the ball. After an athlete is hit with the ball she becomes part of the "it" team. After the "it" team has two or more athletes the "it" person with the ball cannot move. She can throw the ball to a teammate who is also "it," or she can hit an athlete who has not been "tagged" yet. The game continues until the last athlete is tagged.

WRAP-UP
What was important to ensure the "it" team grew in numbers?
Why was it important to rely on your teammates?
How might this apply to our team?

From Karl Rohnke, *Bottomless Baggie* (Kendall/Hunt Publishing: Dubuque, Iowa, 1991).

BALLOON TOWER

GOAL
Reinforce the importance of teamwork and communication.

NUMBERS
No limit.

EQUIPMENT
One or two bags of mixed balloons (100 count).
One roll of masking tape per team.

SPACE
Gymnasium or other hard-surface flooring.

SAFETY
N/A.

GAME PLAN
Creative thinking will be a must for successful completion of this activity. Begin by having team members divide into groups of 3-5. Give each team an equal number of balloons and one roll of masking tape. Inform the teams that they will be competing with the other teams to determine which team can build the tallest balloon tower in the allotted time. The only stipulation for this activity is that the tower must be able to stand without assistance from any team member. Allow each team 5-7 minutes to plan their strategy. Then give them 20 minutes to build their towers.

WRAP-UP
How well did your team use the planning time?
What could you have done to be more efficient?
How well do we use our practice time?
How did your team respond when the activity did not go according to plan?
How might this relate to our team when a game or competition isn't going according to plan?

VARIATIONS
Blindfold a few members of each team, and allow the others to have their sight. Allow only the blindfolded team members to build the tower.

From Karl Rohnke, *Funn Stuff III* (Kendall/Hunt Publishing: Dubuque, Iowa, 1998).

TUG O' WAR

GOAL
Highlight the importance of teamwork and communication.

NUMBERS
No limit, because you will usually have only a certain number on the rope at once and everyone else will be watching.

EQUIPMENT
Large rope at least 30 feet long, two traffic cones, small piece of cloth.

SPACE
Outside on grass or other soft surface.

SAFETY
No horseplay. Avoid having athletes tie the rope around their waists.

GAME PLAN
This activity is conducted like the tug o' war competition that most of us have participated in at one time or another. Divide your team into two smaller equal units. For this activity, it is probably best to put your starters on one team. Teams line up on either end of the rope. Tie a piece of cloth in the middle of the rope and set one traffic cone at about 15 feet on either side of the piece of cloth. On your command, both teams should grab the rope and attempt to pull the opposite team to the cone on their side. A team wins when the lead person from the opposing team is pulled past the cone furthest away. The teams will most likely struggle a while to pull the other team across to their side. On the second attempt have one or two of your starters hold on to the rope without pulling. The result will most likely be that the opposing team will easily pull your starters to their side. This is a great example of what happens when everyone is not doing his part when the team is competing.

WRAP-UP
What was the lesson in this activity?
How might it apply to our situation?
What is it like to put forth a great deal of effort and have a teammate who isn't putting forth much effort?

VARIATIONS
Encourage one of the teams to be vocal in their encouragement and instructions with each other, while forbidding the other team to communicate in any manner. This will highlight the importance and effectiveness of communication.

Contributed by Jay Williams, Former Duke University Men's Basketball Player.

Photo Scavenger Hunt

Goal

Allow athletes the opportunity to get to know one another and encourage teamwork.

Numbers

No limit. Consider dividing team into smaller subunits if more than 10-12 athletes.

Equipment

One disposable camera for each team.
List of requirements or assignments for each team or subunit to fulfill.

Space

A space large enough to make the event challenging (i.e., your campus), but small enough that team members can walk or run everywhere.

Safety

Avoid having athletes use motor vehicles during this activity.

Game Plan

This activity will also work well as an initiative where you are hoping to encourage athletes to get to know each other. Begin by dividing the team into smaller teams of 6-8 athletes. Provide each team with a disposable camera and a list of potential photo opportunities with point values for each photo. Tell the teams they have one hour to take all of the pictures on the list and get the camera back to the coach. Each team member must take at least one of the pictures. Once all teams have finished, you can develop the film and place all pictures on a board (one board per team) and then tally the points. Following is a sample list of pictures your team might take during their scavenger hunt.

School president or principal	5 points
Athletic director	5 points
Picture with a bus driver	5 points
Head football coach	5 points
Picture of a team member sitting at the president's desk	5 points
Picture of the team with the head coach's spouse at his/her place of employment	5 points
Head basketball coach	5 points
Sports editor of the local paper	5 points
Each coach of every other sport	4 points
Sport psychologist	4 points
Assistant athletic directors	3 points
Head equipment manager	3 points
Head of the booster club	3 points
Academic advisor for the team	3 points

Using team members as human letters, spell school name	3 points
Picture of group in front of a school or university landmark	3 points
Picture with favorite food service server	3 points
Picture with each team member hanging on a jungle gym	3 points
Picture of the group with at least 3 random students	3 points

WRAP-UP

What were some of the keys to your team's success?

How important were teamwork and communication?

Did you learn anything new about the people who help us in our quest to be successful?

How might the lessons you learned here apply to our team in a competitive situation?

VARIATION

Have each smaller team take the team's schedule to give to each person they include in their photos, along with a personal invitation to come to the contests. This special invitation may increase your fan attendance!

Contributed by Trip Hedrick, Championship Productions, Ames, Iowa.

PIGPEN

GOAL
Reinforce the importance of teambuilding, trust and team planning.

NUMBERS
8-16 is ideal. Consider dividing team into smaller subunits if more than 16.

EQUIPMENT
20-30 feet of string.
Standards (chairs, goal posts, etc.) on which to tie the string.
A 2" x 6" board, 6-8' long, is optional.
Tumbling mats will be needed if using a hard surface.

SPACE
Area that is free of obstacles and relatively flat.

SAFETY
Have athletes protect their upper bodies when passing from one side to the other.
Remind athletes to always pay attention.
No jumping or throwing athletes through the fence.
No horseplay.

GAME PLAN
This activity will require significant planning on the part of team members. Begin by tying two strings parallel to the ground. One string should be tied at a height that is just below the waist of your tallest athlete. The second string should be tied approximately two feet above the first one. The goal of the activity is for the entire team to move from one side of the pigpen to the other without touching the strings. All team members must pass between the two strings. The team must start over at the beginning if anyone touches either of the strings.

WRAP-UP
Was discussion of a game plan important in this activity? Why or why not?
What were some of the key factors for success in this activity?
If given another chance, what should your team do differently?
How might this activity apply to our team?

VARIATIONS
Use the board as a prop team members can use to help each other move from one side of the fence to the other.
Have the team split into two equal groups and work to get all athletes to the opposite side from where they started.
Allow three touches before requiring the to team start over.
Require only the two most recent athletes to go back to the original side if someone touches a string.

From Karl Rohnke, *Funn Stuff III* (Kendall/Hunt Publishing: Dubuque, Iowa, 1998).

TEAM LUNCHES

GOAL
Allow athletes and coaches to interact in an informal setting.

NUMBERS
No limit.

EQUIPMENT
None.

SPACE
Area where the team can eat lunch together.

SAFETY
N/A.

GAME PLAN
Schedule several dates throughout the season where the entire team eats lunch together. Athletes and coaches should bring their lunches and meet in a specified place such as the locker room, field house, gym, etc. Use this time to talk informally with athletes rather than about the issues of your particular sport.

WRAP-UP
How do you like eating lunch together like this?
Can anyone share something new they learned about a teammate or coach?
Why is it important for us to eat lunch together?
Should we continue it?

VARIATIONS
Have various themes for conversation during lunch. For example, athletes and coaches could be asked to talk about their families, political philosophies, all-time favorite movies, etc.

Have potluck lunches that require all team members to bring something to eat.

Coaches could take passive or active roles in these lunches depending on the goals.

Contributed by Paula Farrell, Athletic Director and Coach, Harford Day School, Bel Air, Maryland.

TEAM DINNERS

GOAL
Encourage teamwork, communication and trust.

NUMBERS
No limit.

EQUIPMENT
Enough food to feed everyone.

SPACE
Your house.

SAFETY
N/A.

GAME PLAN
Plan at least one night where your team can come to your house to eat dinner. This is a great opportunity for your athletes to see you as a person outside of your role as their coach. You can have the entire team come to dinner or break the team into smaller groups to allow for more interaction with each athlete. If your team is small enough, it would be great if you also had athletes over for dinner one at a time. It is important that this time is spent discussing topics other than the team or the sport.

WRAP-UP
You can get informal and/or formal feedback from your athletes about the effectiveness of this activity by simply asking them personally or including it on an end-of-year evaluation.

VARIATIONS
Have the team cook the meal.

Include the entire team if you have a small team or divide the team into subunits and have each subunit responsible for a portion of the meal (e.g., appetizer, main course, side dishes, dessert, etc.).

Require the team or each subunit to work together on every aspect of the preparation of their portion of the meal. This could include buying the ingredients, preparing the food and traveling together to the dinner.

A different variation would be to eat at a restaurant with athletes from different subunits or classes (e.g., sophomores, juniors etc.).

TEAM ROAD RACES

GOAL
Allow athletes to see teammates in a setting outside your sport.
Encourage teamwork among team members.
Highlight the importance of sport relative to life issues.

NUMBERS
No limit.

EQUIPMENT
Running shoes.

SPACE
Designated course.

SAFETY
Injured athletes should not be forced to participate as runners, but they could be there to cheer on teammates or hand out water, etc.

GAME PLAN
This is a great teambuilding activity that also helps athletes see the "bigger picture" when it comes to life. Find a local road race that your entire team can participate in at some point during the year. It might be preferable to find a race that is sponsoring a cause—for example, cancer research or building of a children's hospital, etc. This race doesn't have to be a competition among teammates and shouldn't be looked upon as a "workout." It should be considered a teambuilding experience where athletes can enjoy themselves and feel as if they are making a difference in a cause greater than themselves. You can eat a meal together afterwards and spend time discussing the particular cause they helped sponsor.

WRAP-UP
Did you enjoy participating in the race?
How does it feel to know you helped a cause or benefit for a different group?
Why is it important to keep causes like this in mind as we go through everyday life?

VARIATIONS
Allow athletes to choose a race to participate in as subunits.
Have one practice where everyone wears the T-shirt they received when running the race.

Contributed by Paula Farrell, Athletic Director and Coach, Harford Day School, Bel Air, Maryland.

TEAM TRANSPORT

GOAL
Reinforce the importance of communication and teamwork.

NUMBERS
6-18 is ideal. Consider dividing athletes into smaller subunits if more than 18.

EQUIPMENT
One regular bath towel or burlap bag per 6 athletes.
Adjust the number of athletes per towel, depending on the physical size of the athletes (e.g., more athletes per towel if they are smaller).

SPACE
A gymnasium floor or any other smooth surface that will allow athletes to slide towels while standing on them.

SAFETY
No horseplay.

GAME PLAN
Place one towel per 6 athletes next to each other on the baseline or designated line to begin the activity. Have athletes take their shoes and socks off before beginning. The objective for this activity is for the entire team to stand on the towels and advance to a designated line about 30 feet away. The following rules should be followed:

> Each athlete must have both feet in contact with a towel at all times.

> No other body part may touch a towel.

> No part of anyone's foot may touch the floor.

> The entire team must maintain contact by either interlocking arms or holding hands. Therefore, groups of athletes on different towels must be connected somehow.

If any of these rules are not followed, the entire team must start over from the beginning.

WRAP-UP
What was the most difficult part of this activity?
What were the responses of team members when you were told the task?
Are there situations that happen during practice or competition where athletes might have a similar response? What is a more appropriate response?
Did anyone become frustrated? What is the most appropriate way to deal with frustration?

VARIATIONS
Blindfold several of the athletes to increase the difficulty and reliance on each other.
Have every other athlete face in the opposite direction to increase the difficulty.
Have subunits compete with each other or put a time limit on it to make it more competitive.

YOU WANT *HOW MUCH* PLAYING TIME?

GOAL
Illustrate the importance of team members accepting their roles on the team.

NUMBERS
No limit.

EQUIPMENT
One piece of paper and pencil for each athlete.

SPACE
Locker room or classroom where team members will not be disturbed.

SAFETY
N/A.

GAME PLAN
This activity will help athletes see that everyone cannot play the exact role they would like. Begin by giving each team member a slip of paper and pencil. Inform them that you are interested in getting their feedback on how much playing time each of them would like to have during a game or competition. Have each athlete write down how many minutes per contest he feels he should average during the season. Collect the slips of paper once everyone has written the number of minutes. Without revealing any names, write each person's number of minutes where everyone can see them. Then add all the minutes together and write the total for everyone to see. Obviously, you will have many more minutes on the board than there are minutes in a game or competition. This is where you can begin to discuss the shortage of available playing time and how it is impossible to satisfy everyone on the team. This will provide a good introduction into the importance of everyone playing a certain role to ensure the team's success.

WRAP-UP
Were any of you surprised at the number of minutes we would have to have available to satisfy everyone?

What should team members do when they feel they are not getting the playing time they feel they deserve?

How can we get everyone to "buy into" their roles on the team?

Contributed by Denny Kuiper, Sports Communication Consultant, Raleigh, NC.

TEAM LIMBO

GOAL
Reinforce the importance of teamwork in a challenging situation.

NUMBERS
No limit. Consider dividing athletes into smaller subunits if more than 15.

EQUIPMENT
Limbo stick (pole-vault pole, high-jump bar, cane pole etc.) or string.

SPACE
Any surface that is free of obstacles or sharp objects.

SAFETY
No horseplay of any kind during this activity.

GAME PLAN
Athletes will enjoy this activity, as it is very similar to the dance many of them have attempted in the past. Begin by having two people hold the limbo stick at about three feet off the ground. If using string, you can tie it to two stationary objects at that height. The goal is for the entire team to go under the stick to the opposite side without anyone touching the stick. Here are a few rules the athletes must follow:

> The only part of an athlete's body that can touch the ground is his or her feet.

> Athletes can go under the stick using any style they wish.

> Once an athlete moves under the stick, he or she can't go back to the other side without going back under the stick.

> If anyone touches the floor with any body part other than the feet or anyone touches the stick, the entire team must start over.

> Teammates are allowed to help each other.

WRAP-UP
What did you learn from this activity?
Were all of you able to go from one side to the other on your own?
What was it like for those of you that needed help?
What types of situations might arise for this team where some might have a difficult time and need the help of their teammates?

VARIATIONS
Lower the stick or string if this is too easy for the team.
Blindfold a few of the team members before the activity begins.

From Alana Jones, *Team Building Activities for Every Group* (Rec Room Publishing: Richland, Washington, 1999).

SERVICE PROJECT

GOAL
Reinforce the importance of teamwork and help athletes appreciate their situations compared to those less fortunate.

NUMBERS
No limit.

EQUIPMENT
None.

SPACE
Will depend on where you conduct the activity.

SAFETY
N/A.

GAME PLAN
This is a simple but very effective activity. It will take some advanced work on your part, but it will be well worth your time. There are countless opportunities for your team to become involved in a cause or organization in your community or surrounding area. Examples of service projects that teams have been involved with include reading with children at elementary schools, feeding the homeless at a shelter, assisting with Special Olympics events, visiting children in the hospital, and conducting a free instructional clinic for local youth, to name just a few. You could provide several service opportunities from which team members could choose, or you could assign one that you feel will be most beneficial for the organization and your team. The key is to get the team involved in a purpose that is "bigger than the team."

WRAP-UP
What was that experience like for you?
What lessons did you take from this experience?
Does it provide you with a different perspective? Why or why not?

POTATO RELAY

GOAL

Encourage teamwork and the ability to laugh at oneself.

NUMBERS

No limit. Divide larger team into smaller subunits.

EQUIPMENT

One potato, one chair and one bucket per team.

SPACE

Area large enough to place chairs about 20-30 feet apart.

SAFETY

No horseplay.

GAME PLAN

Team members will most certainly laugh at themselves and along with their teammates during this activity. Begin by placing the chairs on one end and buckets on the other end about 20-30 feet apart. Have each team line up behind a chair and place the potato on the chair. The objective of this game is that on the start signal, the first athlete in line must bend down and pick up the potato between her legs and run to the bucket with the potato between her legs. Once she arrives at the bucket, she is to drop it into the bucket. Then she reaches into the bucket, picks it up with her hands and runs back to her team and places the potato on the chair for the next teammate. Each teammate does the same thing until the last person in line places the potato back on the chair. An athlete must take the potato back to the chair and begin again if she drops it or touches it with any part of her body other than her legs on the way to dropping it in the bucket.

WRAP-UP

How did you feel while carrying the potato between your legs?

Why is it important to be able to laugh at yourself and not worry about what you look like while trying to accomplish a task?

How did you feel when one of your teammates had to start over because she dropped the potato or touched it with a different part of her body?

What is the best way to respond to mistakes by teammates?

Contributed by Nicole Detling, Sport Psychology doctoral student, University of Utah.

WATER RELAY

GOAL
Encourage teamwork among subunits or small groups on a team.

NUMBERS
No limit. Divide larger teams into smaller subunits or teams.

EQUIPMENT
One 2-gallon bucket, one 1-gallon bucket and 16-ounce cup for each subunit or team.
Enough water to fill all 2-gallon buckets.

SPACE
Outdoor setting because of the water involved.

SAFETY
N/A.

GAME PLAN
Divide the team into equal smaller teams or subunits. Place the 2-gallon buckets in a line, 10-15 feet apart. Have teams line up behind their respective buckets at arm's length between each athlete. Then place the 1-gallon buckets at the opposite end of each line. Each of the 1-gallon buckets should have a fill line marked on the inside at the exact same level. Fill the 2-gallon buckets with water. The object of this activity is for each team to fill the 1-gallon bucket to the marked line with water by passing water from the 2-gallon bucket with the 16-ounce cup. This is done in an assembly line fashion, with each athlete passing the cup. The winning team is the one that can fill the 1-gallon bucket to the fill line the fastest.

WRAP-UP
Did your team have a particular strategy?
How important was communication in this activity?

VARIATIONS
Team members could be blindfolded. Team members could be required to run some distance before handing the 16-ounce cup to the next teammate.

TISSUE RACE

GOAL
Encourage teamwork and fun in a relay situation.

NUMBERS
8-20 is ideal.

EQUIPMENT
One spoon and one tissue for each athlete.
Two chairs for each team or subunit.
One small bucket or bag.

SPACE
Area half the size of a basketball court.

SAFETY
No horseplay.

GAME PLAN
Team members will enjoy this seemingly simple but challenging activity. Begin by placing two chairs about 30-40 feet apart. Place the small bag or bucket on one of the chairs. Divide your team into smaller teams or subunits of 4-6 athletes, and have each team or subunit line up behind the chair without the bucket or bag on it. Have the first athlete place a tissue on the chair. The objective is for the athlete to pick up the tissue with a spoon and race the tissue as quickly as possible and drop it into the small bucket or bag on the other chair. Once he has done that, he runs back to the next athlete, who then puts his tissue on the chair and attempts to pick it up with his spoon and repeat the process. The winning team is the one where all athletes run the course first. While running with the spoon and tissue, the athlete is not allowed to touch the tissue with anything but the spoon. If he touches it or drops it to the ground, he must run back to the original chair and start the race over again.

WRAP-UP
Did you have fun with this activity?
What was the key to successfully accomplishing the task?
What was it like when one of your teammates dropped the tissue or had to start over for some reason?
Will your teammates ever make mistakes during the season?
What is the best way to handle those mistakes as a teammate?

Contributed by Nicole Detling, Sport Psychology doctoral student, University of Utah.

Banana Relay

Goal
Encourage teamwork and communication among team members.

Numbers
8-10 is ideal. Divide the team into smaller subunits if larger than 10.

Equipment
One banana for each team or subunit.

Space
Area about a quarter the size of a basketball court.

Safety
No horseplay.
Make sure no athletes are allergic to bananas.

Game Plan
Begin this activity by having each team sit down in a line so that everyone is facing the front of the line. Make sure the person who is sitting at the front of the line is someone who likes to eat bananas. Once everyone is in place, the first person in each line must put the banana between his feet. On the signal, the first athlete in each line should roll or somersault backwards toward the next teammate in line while keeping the banana between his feet. The first athlete is attempting to pass the banana to the second athlete's feet. The second athlete must then roll backwards and pass it to the third athlete's feet. This sequence continues until it reaches the last athlete in line. Once he receives the banana in his feet, he must spin around and start the sequence over again in the opposite direction. When the banana reaches the athlete who began the activity, he must then peel it and eat it as quickly as possible. The winning team is determined by who can eat the banana and then be the first to whistle out loud. If an athlete drops the banana or touches it with any body part other than his feet, the banana must go back to the person who began that sequence, and it starts over. It is very likely the banana will be mushy by the time it reaches the beginning again.

Wrap-Up
What was the most difficult part of this activity?
Did you have to communicate with each other during the activity?
How did you feel when one of your teammates dropped the banana or caused the team to start over for some reason?
What is the best way for us to respond to mistakes made by teammates?

Contributed by Nicole Detling, Sport Psychology doctoral student, University of Utah.

INCHWORM RELAY

GOAL
Emphasize the importance of teamwork and communication.

NUMBERS
12 or more is ideal.

EQUIPMENT
None.

SPACE
A smooth floor about half the size of a basketball court.

SAFETY
No horseplay.

GAME PLAN
Begin this activity by explaining to your athletes there will be many times they will have to work effectively in unison. This activity will challenge them to work in unison in order to be successful. Divide athletes into equal teams with at least five on each team. Once the athletes have been divided into teams, have them sit in a line on the floor with their feet on the athlete's lap in front of them. The first athlete in line is allowed to put his feet on the floor and the last athlete is allowed to put his hands on the floor. No one else is allowed to put his hands or feet on the floor. The objective for this activity is for each team to move from the starting point to a designated stopping point as quickly as possible without making a mistake. Each athlete must roll his rear end back and forth in unison with the other members of the team while inching forward. A team must go back to the start if anyone on the team other than the first and last athlete touches the floor or breaks contact with the athlete in front of him. The team that wins is the one that covers the distance the quickest.

WRAP-UP
What happened during this activity?
How important was it to work together during this activity?
When is it important for us to work together as a team?
What do we need to do if we are not working together well as a team?

HOOP RELAY

GAME PLAN
Emphasize the importance of teamwork and communication.

NUMBERS
12 or more is ideal.

EQUIPMENT
Enough Hula Hoops for each team to have one.

SPACE
An area large enough to have lines of at least 6 people and space to move around the lines.

SAFETY
No horseplay.

GAME PLAN
Team members will be able to laugh at themselves and see the importance of communication and teamwork while participating in this activity. Begin by having teams of athletes form single-file lines with one Hula Hoop at the front of each line. Tell the first athlete in line to reach between her legs and hold a hand of the second athlete, who reaches her other hand between her legs to the third person, who reaches her free hand between her legs. This continues until the entire team is in a line with hands joined between their legs, and the only athletes with free hands are the first and last ones in line. The race begins when the first athlete picks up the Hula Hoop with her free hand and steps through the hoop. Then the objective becomes to get the entire team through the hoop while holding hands. When the last athlete passes through the hoop, she lets go of the athlete's hand in front of her and carries the hoop to the front of the line and reaches a free hand through her legs and joins hands with the athlete behind her and the process begins over again. This continues until the entire team has a chance to be at the front of the line once. If team members lose contact with each other by dropping hands, the hoop must be sent back to the beginning of the line and the sequence starts over with the athlete who is at the front of the line when contact is lost.

WRAP-UP
What was the key to being successful in this activity?
Was there anything difficult about this activity?
Is it important for our team to work together like this? If so, why?

From Karl Rohnke, *Silver Bullets* (Project Adventure, Inc.: Beverly, MA, 1984).

POTATO CHIP RELAY

GOAL
Encourage teamwork during conditioning.

NUMBERS
No limit.

EQUIPMENT
Bag of potato chips.

SPACE
Any space where you typically conduct conditioning.

SAFETY
N/A.

GAME PLAN
This activity will allow your athletes to have a little fun while conditioning. They will work hard and hardly notice they are working. Divide the athletes on your team into equal smaller teams or subunits. Each team should be given one potato chip. The object of this activity is for each team member to run a designated distance or course and then hand the chip to the next person in line. The winning team is the team who can finish first without any damage to the potato chip. Have some type of reward for the winning team.

WRAP-UP
You may want to wait for them to catch their breath after this one.
How did teamwork come into play during this activity?
Are there times in our sport where you have to concentrate when you are fatigued?
What is the best way to handle that situation?

VARIATIONS
This activity can be done with almost any conditioning drill you use.

BELLY BALL RELAY

GOAL
Encourage teamwork among pairs of athletes.

NUMBERS
12 or more is ideal.

EQUIPMENT
Beach balls, basketballs or a ball similar in size.
An object for teams to race around, such as a cone or pole.

SPACE
An area about the size of half of a basketball court.

SAFETY
Flat area that is free of obstacles.

GAME PLAN
This is an excellent opportunity to encourage teamwork among athletes who might be currently experiencing difficulties getting along with each other. Begin by dividing the team into two or more teams of at least six athletes. Have athletes get into pairs once teams have been established. Make sure you have a start/finish line and an object for the athletes to race around and back to the team. Place one ball on the ground in front of each team. The first pair on each team should move to either side of the ball and get ready to start. The object of the relay is for the first pair from each team to work together to pick up the ball without using their arms or hands and carry it around the cone and back to the next pair waiting at the start/finish line. Each pair must follow one basic rule during this activity: arms and hands cannot touch the ball at any time during the race. If the ball is touched with arms or hands of any athlete at any time, the ball must be placed on the ground where the infraction occurred and the pair must pick the ball up again and continue. Someone should serve as a referee to monitor the pairs and ensure fair play from everyone. Athletes should be reminded that the only way to move the ball forward is to carry it between athletes.

WRAP-UP
What was the key to success for this activity?
How much did you depend on your partner for success?
Are there times when we need to depend on another person on our team?

VARIATIONS
Make a rule that each pair must have their hands on their heads when carrying the ball.

TEAM OLYMPICS

GOAL
Encourage teamwork, communication and pride within subunits on your team.

NUMBERS
No limit. The larger the better, but you will need to divide the team into smaller subunits of at least six athletes.

EQUIPMENT
Depends on the activities you decide to include in the competition.

SPACE
An area that is large enough to field all of the events and is free of any obstacles.

SAFETY
No horseplay.

Plan activities where athletes are not likely to be injured.

GAME PLAN
This activity can be a very nice change of pace for your athletes. It has been successfully carried out in the preseason and during the off-season, but depending on your sport, it could be successfully carried out at some point during the season as well. This activity is carried out in much the same way as the traditional field day at elementary schools. You can select a series of activities from this book where subunits compete with each other for a point total. Allow team members to wear team colors. Keep score for each of the events and have an award for the winning team. That team can be allowed to keep the award until the next field day, when it is passed on to the next winning team. The award doesn't have to be significant for the subunits to covet it. It will soon become an award they take pride in and compete to earn. Your athletes will have fun and compete at the same time.

WRAP-UP
What was it like to compete with your subunit?

What allowed you to be successful or caused you to be unsuccessful?

How do you have to depend on the other athletes within your subunit on our team?

VARIATIONS
Make teams that comprise athletes from different positions or classes if there is a need to allow athletes from different positions to get to know one another better.

Incorporate coaches into the teams according to the subunits they coach.

Adventure-Based Activities

The following five activities are somewhat different from the other activities highlighted in this book. They are adventure-based activities, which implies they most often take place in the wilderness. Therefore, you will have to take your team to a location away from campus. Athletes that participate in these types of programs are challenged to take risks and effectively deal with many unknown factors. It is very important that you secure the services of qualified and well-trained facilitators to take you and your team through these experiences. You should never attempt to take your team through these activities on your own. The activities we will describe are high ropes course, white-water rafting, overnight camping trip, hiking or mountain climbing, and a caving experience.

HIGH ROPES

GOAL
Encourage athletes to overcome fear and encourage trust among team members.

NUMBERS
No limit. Consider dividing the team into smaller subunits if more than 20.

EQUIPMENT
All equipment should be provided by the company running the ropes course.

SPACE
High ropes facility.

SAFETY
Follow all rules stipulated by the facilitators. Make sure the facilitators taking you through this activity are trained by an ACCT (Association for Challenge Course Technology) vendor company and the course is inspected by an ACCT vendor. To find an ACCT course near you, go to **www.acct.org** or contact the authors.

GAME PLAN
This is an excellent activity if you want to challenge your athletes to extend their comfort zones as well as enhance trust among teammates. The high ropes course can also help enhance the confidence of your athletes by helping them overcome negative thoughts and worries about failure. Participants on a high ropes course are put in what is perceived to be a "dangerous" situation, but is in reality very safe. Athletes are required to climb to a height that ranges from 20 to 50 feet while wearing the appropriate safety equipment. This is a difficult and frightening experience for some athletes. However, encouragement and support from teammates will serve to help participants navigate the high course successfully. Team members will feel a sense of accomplishment and this experience will be one they can relate to throughout the season when adversity comes.

WRAP-UP
What was that experience like for each of you?
How many of you were honestly scared at one point?
How did your teammates help you through the course?
How can this be applied to our team and the experiences we will have throughout the year?

CAMPING TRIP

GOAL
Allow your team to experience a certain level of adversity and work together to overcome that adversity.

NUMBERS
Only limited by the amount of camping equipment you can secure.

EQUIPMENT
Camping equipment.

SPACE
Any camping space that is considered safe.

SAFETY
Precaution should be taken to avoid exposure to extreme conditions. Your trainer or team physician should make the trip with you.

GAME PLAN
This can be one of the most powerful activities you ever do with a team. It can be especially effective with a team that has a difficult time handling adversity. Taking your team on a camping trip has the potential to provide you and your team with valuable insight into how athletes will respond to a situation that is beyond the comfort zone for many of them. It is important to have the entire team involved in as many of the activities as possible during the trip. You could have team members work with each other on tasks such as gathering firewood, building a fire, cooking food and setting up the campsite.

WRAP-UP
How did you like camping?

Was it outside your comfort zone?

Will there be times when you or our team has to extend our comfort zones and perform well?

Did we face any adversity? If so, what was the initial response? What is the best way for us to handle adversity?

VARIATION
Without letting anyone else know about it, purposely leave the tents behind. This will provide an excellent opportunity to see the response and the process the team might go through to overcome this adversity. It has the potential to provide a very real experience the team will refer back to throughout the season. In essence it can help them realize they can effectively handle any adversity they might face.

Rather than leaving the tents behind, you can create other, more adverse situations on the trip. Of course this should be done with the overall safety of all of your athletes in mind.

HIKING OR MOUNTAIN CLIMBING

GOAL
Reinforce the importance of teamwork, communication and trust among team members and challenge athletes to extend their comfort zones.

NUMBERS
No limit. Consider dividing team into smaller subunits if you have a large team.

EQUIPMENT
The company you contract with should provide a list of equipment each participant should bring on the trip.

SPACE
Mountain or other challenging terrain.

SAFETY
It is imperative that everyone participating in this activity follows all rules and regulations stipulated by the contracting company.

GAME PLAN
This is an excellent activity to encourage athletes to rise to a challenge and depend on teammates in a variety of ways. As stated before, it is important to utilize the services of a qualified guide to take you through this activity. Keeping in mind the safety of your athletes, climbing a mountain of minimum to medium difficulty would be ideal. However, taking a long hike that is somewhat difficult will also reveal a great deal about your team and provide an excellent avenue for athletes to learn more about how they handle adversity. To begin this activity you could help your athletes see how climbing a mountain is like the team's ultimate goal at the end of the season. Encourage them to discuss what they think it will take to climb the mountain and how those things relate to what the team must do during the season to be successful. Once you begin the ascent, it is important to take note of how athletes respond to various obstacles and challenges. Observe whether athletes stay together during the climb or whether some athletes surge ahead of the group and others fall behind. At some point during the climb, you can require the group to stay together by having each athlete serve as the lead person for a short period of time and then fall to the back of the line. This sequence would continue until the first athlete is back to the front of the line. You can stop the team along the way and ask whether they are maintaining positive attitudes and communicating with each other. Upon reaching the summit, allow athletes to spend time enjoying the view and encourage them to reflect on their roles on this climb and their roles on the team. You can also use this time to have athletes reflect on questions such as, "What are the strengths of this team?" "Do we utilize these strengths as well as we should?" "Do we have areas that will keep us from achieving our goals if left unchecked?" Bring the team together and discuss these issues before beginning your descent. Observe the same types of situations on the way down and see if the team improved or changed anything.

WRAP-UP

Was anyone apprehensive about this activity in any way before we began?

Were any of you challenged to extend your comfort zones? If so, how?

How important were teamwork and communication in this activity?

Were there times when we were "together" as a team and times when we seemed to be "splintered" as a team?

Did you have to trust your teammates at any point?

How can this activity be applied to what we must do to accomplish our team goals?

VARIATIONS

This experience could be tied to a camping trip like the one discussed in this section.

WHITE-WATER RAFTING

GOAL
Reinforce the importance of teamwork, communication and trust among team members, as well challenging athletes to extend their comfort zones.

NUMBERS
No limit.

EQUIPMENT
The company you contract with should provide a list of equipment each participant should bring on the trip.

SPACE
River.

SAFETY
It is imperative that everyone participating in this activity follows all rules and regulations stipulated by the contracting company.

GAME PLAN
Many of the athletes on your team have likely never experienced a white-water rafting experience. Hopefully, this experience will be fun and at the same time challenge them to overcome their fear of the unknown. This activity can be conducted as a single event or can be combined with other adventure activities mentioned in this book. It is imperative that a certified outfitter company is used when conducting this activity. To find qualified white-water rafting outfitters near you, go to **www.rafting.com.** To make the experience more challenging, utilize the services of a company that uses a river with Class III or higher rapids.

WRAP-UP
What were some of the experiences the team shared on the river?

How did you and your teammates react after experiencing a big rapid on the river?

What lessons can you take from this experience and apply to what we have to do in our sport to be successful?

CAVING EXPERIENCE

GOAL
Reinforce the importance of teamwork, communication and trust among team members, and challenge them to extend their comfort zones and overcome fear.

NUMBERS
No limit.

EQUIPMENT
The company you contract with should provide a list of equipment each participant should bring on the trip.

SPACE
Cavern or cave.

SAFETY
It is imperative that everyone participating in this activity follows all rules and regulations stipulated by the contracting company.

GAME PLAN
This is an excellent activity for challenging athletes to move beyond their comfort zones and depend on their teammates to accomplish what might be perceived as a very difficult task. Athletes will likely be challenged to rock climb in the dark, crawl through small holes and traverse over deep gaps in the earth while caving. As with the other adventure-based activities, it is imperative that you utilize the services of a qualified professional to lead your team on a caving experience. It is very likely that many of your athletes have never experienced an activity similar to this one. So before beginning, ask your athletes to discuss the types of obstacles and challenges they might face while participating in this activity. Athletes will most likely be assigned a "buddy" for safety. They will have to rely on this person throughout this experience. As a result, it might be beneficial to separate cliques on the team and even assign partners so that athletes who don't necessarily get along well have to work together. You will have numerous opportunities to ask athletes how their experiences during this activity relate to their sport and the importance of depending on each other for success.

WRAP-UP
Was anyone apprehensive about this activity in any way before we began?
Were any of you challenged to extend your comfort zones? If so, how?
How important were teamwork and communication in this activity?
How important was your partner during this activity?
How can this activity be applied to what we must do to accomplish our team goals?

VARIATIONS
This experience could be tied to a camping trip like the one discussed in this section.

From Ian Boyle, *The Impact of Adventure-Based Training on Team Cohesion and Psychological Skills Development in Elite Sporting Teams* (**dissertation.com**: USA, 2002).

Coaching Staff Activities

RETREATS

A retreat is an excellent activity to do with your staff during the pre- or post-season depending on your objective. As with the retreat with the entire team mentioned earlier in this book, the coaching staff could take a few days together somewhere away from the office. This time can be used to challenge the staff to grow in terms of their professional development or simply prepare for the upcoming season. Coaching staffs that have done this before have focused on such areas as goals for the team and coaching staff for the year, team environment and team rules, as well as defining roles for the staff and athletes. Your staff will appreciate the opportunity to develop camaraderie while outlining the upcoming season.

ROPES COURSE

As with your athletes, this is an excellent activity if you want to challenge members of the coaching staff to extend their comfort zones as well as enhance trust among colleagues. Just as you ask athletes to extend their comfort zones, a ropes course will require the coaches on your staff to do tasks that are challenging and sometimes fear-provoking. They will certainly be required to depend on each other. Like athletes on the team, coaches will feel a sense of accomplishment and this experience will be one they can relate to throughout the season when adversity comes. Be sure you have a certified instructor and facilitator to take your staff through this process. Go to **www.acct.org** to find a ropes course and certified instructor near you.

SWITCH POSITIONS

There is certainly something to say for the old adage, "If it ain't broke, don't fix it." And the coaches on your staff might very well be as motivated and innovative as they were when they first began coaching. One potential downfall of a staff working together for a long period of time is that some coaches could become "too comfortable" in their positions. If this becomes a problem, you might consider having the coaches on your staff change positions with each other. For example, the Women's Basketball staff at Duke University changed positions with each other after being together and coaching the same positions for twelve years. The coach that was responsible for the post players began coaching the guards and vice versa. The coaches on that staff embraced the change as a challenge and it helped them become even better students of the game.

Switch Teams

This idea is relevant for you if you have a feeder program. On occasion, you and your coaching staff could switch teams that you coach. For example, in Dave Archer's unpublished manuscript, *Beyond the Xs and Os,* the author encourages members of the varsity staff to spend a day coaching one of the lower-level teams, and those coaches can then spend time with the varsity team. You could limit the number of coaches that switch teams at any one time to alleviate any concern over lost productivity. An exercise such as this might provide coaches a deeper appreciation for those who coach at different levels. It will also serve as a motivator for athletes playing at the lower levels.

Family Night

Coaching takes significant time and energy, regardless of the level or sport you coach. The relationship between a coach and his or her family can often become strained during a season because of the lack of quality time spent together. One activity you can do as a staff is have "family night" once a week during the season. Have the entire staff bring their families to the office one night a week. You can have a meal catered or have members of your booster club take turns cooking it. This will not only help with the camaraderie of your staff, but it will increase camaraderie among families of the coaches. Also, Tom Osborne, the legendary former football coach at the University of Nebraska, saved Wednesday nights during the season as "date night" with his wife. This was a way for him to make sure he spent quality time with his wife during the hectic season.

Treat Members of Staff with Respect

One of the biggest mistakes head coaches make is to embarrass a member of the staff in front of the athletes or other staff members. It is important to remember that none of the coaches on your staff intentionally make mistakes. Think about your response if your athletic director embarrassed or belittled you in front of your peers. It would make it difficult for you to respect that person and have an effective working relationship him or her. Always discuss disagreements behind closed doors, or in a manner that doesn't single out one coach in front of others. They will respect you much more and be willing to go the extra mile when you ask it of them.

ALLOW THE STAFF TO PROVIDE YOU WITH FEEDBACK

Often in the coaching profession, people are hired because of a past relationship with the head coach. Sometimes this is a very good situation, and other times it is not because the assistant coaches have a difficult time being honest with the head coach. If you are a head coach, it is imperative that you create an environment where your assistant coaches can provide you with feedback regarding your overall leadership skills. The ideal situation would be for you to provide them the opportunity to provide feedback in one-on-one conversations. Or, you can design a form they can fill out in an anonymous manner. If you have individual conversations with the staff, it is important to conduct these meetings someplace other than your office. For example, you can do it over a meal or in their offices. This will put them more at ease and they will be more willing to be honest with you. Either way you decide to do this activity, it is necessary for you to take the feedback, learn from it, change those areas you feel will help the team and avoid holding grudges against your staff. If you hold grudges, no one will be honest with you in the future.

Conclusion

We hope we have provided you with a few activities you can use with your team and coaching staff to emphasize various aspects of the team process. As we indicated in the introduction, some of these activities will require you and your coaches to move beyond your comfort zones in order to try them. They will certainly challenge many of your athletes to extend their comfort zones. However, as you probably know by now, the benefits of incorporating experiential activities in your repertoire of teaching and coaching tools can be very beneficial.

Remember to always keep your athletes' perspectives in mind as you take them through these activities. By doing this, you will allow them to get maximum benefit from participating, and your team will have a much better chance of working well together as well as communicating with and trusting each other in competitive situations. Best of luck in your attempts to develop these very important aspects of team success!

About the Authors

About Greg Dale

Gregory A. Dale, Ph.D. is a Professor of Sport Psychology and Sport Ethics at Duke University. He is also Director of the Sport Psychology and Leadership Programs for Duke Athletics. In addition to his work with Duke athletes and coaches, Greg consults with numerous college and professional athletes and teams. He also consults with corporations around the world including The World Bank, Habitat for Humanity International, Pfizer and SKANSKA International. Greg has written four books related to leadership and performance. In addition, he has written scripts and served as the "expert" on a series of thirteen videos for coaches, athletes and parents. Greg has been featured on Good Morning America, ESPN, MSNBC, Court TV and numerous national radio programs. He is also a member of the Sport Psychology Staff for USA Track and Field.

About Scott Conant

Scott Conant is the Director of Training for Signature Research Inc., a full service challenge course company. Scott joined the Signature Research Inc. team after teaching more than 20 years at Winthrop University in the Department of Physical Education, Sport, and Human Performance. He managed the University's challenge course program with the responsibilities of lead facilitator, staff training, marketing, and maintenance. He is a former All-American basketball player, team captain, and played professionally in Europe after being drafted by the New York Nets of the National Basketball Association. He has coached at the university, high school, and kid's league levels.

Scott is active in community service and was a member of the York County Sports Council. He is a former editor and past chair of the Association for Experiential Education Southeast Region. He was a member of the Association for Challenge Course Technology implementation task force which introduced facilitation standards to the challenge course industry.

Scott has presented at state, regional, and international conferences and presents teambuilding workshops throughout the world.

Scott can be contacted for teambuilding workshops and training at dsconant@gmail.com or through signatureresearch.com.

Workshops by Greg Dale

Developing the Credible Coach: A Model for Success

This workshop is based on Dr. Dale's book, *The Seven Secrets of Successful Coaches: How to Unlock and Unleash Your Team's Full Potential* and is geared towards coaches. It emphasizes the importance of earning credibility with athletes as well as the dynamics of group development and productivity. Numerous recommendations are made to build effective leadership skills while also building high-performing teams.

Maximizing Your Potential: A Model for Performance Excellence

This workshop challenges athletes to extend their comfort zones and critically examine their approach to excellence. Topics covered in this workshop include preparing for success, embracing the pressure, trusting your instincts, effective goal-setting, perseverance in difficult situations and leadership skills. Application of these skills to areas outside of athletics is reinforced throughout the presentation.

The Sport Parent: Helping Your Athlete Maximize His or Her Potential

Parents play a crucial role in determining whether or not children have a positive experience in sport. This thought-provoking workshop encourages parents to analyze the type of environment they are creating for their children. Topics covered in this workshop include the significance of the coach-athlete-parent triangle, lessons parents want children to learn from sport and the importance of modeling those lessons and effective goal-setting that parents can use with their children.

Teambuilding 101: Keys to Enhancing Teamwork, Communication and Trust

This interactive workshop provides athletes on a team with practical activities they can use to enhance team cohesion. Specifically, athletes will have an opportunity to experience several activities that promote teamwork, communication, trust and positive team culture.

140

Coach, Athlete and Parent Products

Books

The Seven Secrets of Successful Coaches: How to Unlock and Unleash Your Team's Full Potential—$29.95

The Fulfilling Ride: A Parent's Guide to Helping Athletes Have a Successful Sport Experience—$9.95

It's a Mental Thing: Five Keys to Improving Performance and Enjoying Sport—$14.95 (Available Spring 2010)

DVDs for Coaches

The Coach's Guide to Developing Great Captains—$39.95 **(NEW)**
Goal Setting for Success: A Coach's Guide—$39.95
The Coach's Guide To Team Building—$39.95
Coaching the Perfectionist Athlete—$39.95
Developing Confident Athletes: A Coach's Guide—$39.95
The Coach's Guide to Dealing Effectively With Parents—$39.95
The Coach's Guide to Team Building Volume II—$39.95

DVDs for Athletes

The Team Captain's Guide to Great Leadership—$39.95 **(NEW)**
Becoming a Champion Athlete: Making Every Practice Count—$29.95
Becoming a Champion Athlete: Mastering Pressure Situations—$29.95
Becoming a Champion Athlete: Goal Setting for Success—$29.95
Becoming a Champion: An Athlete's Guide to Building Self-Confidence—$29.95

DVDs for Parents

Promoting a Positive Athletic Experience: The Parent's Guide—$39.95

Visit www.excellenceinperformance.com or call 919-401-9640

101 Teambuilding Activities:
Ideas Every Coach Can Use to Enhance Teamwork, Communication and Trust

Greg Dale and Scott Conant

To order additional copies of this book
Call: **919-401-9640**
Visit: **www.excellenceinperformance.com**
Or mail check, money order, or credit card information to:

Excellence in Performance
7 Sinclair Circle
Durham, NC 27705

Name _____

School _____

Sport _____

Address _____

City, State, Zip _____

Country _____

Phone _____

E-mail _____

Credit Card _____

Exp. _____